THE VAPOR

Transform Your Life With An Eternal Perspective

XOLA MALIK

THE VAPOR

Copyright © 2012 by Xola Malik

Request for information should be addressed to:
Xola Malik
booking4xola@gmail.com
www.thevaporbook.com
www.xolamusic.com

All rights reserved. No part of this publication may be reproduced, stored in a retrieval system, or transmitted in any form or by any means electronic, mechanical, photocopy, recording, or other—without the prior written permission from the Publisher.

Contributing Editors: Carmen Watson, Liz L. Fernandez
Cover design & layout: Liz L. Fernandez

Published by Xola Malik
www.thevaporbook.com

ISBN 978-1-62030-182-1

Printed and bound in the United States of America.

DEDICATION

I dedicate this book to the amazing
Micaiah, Marquis, Monet, and Mattias.
God has truly blessed my life with your presence.

TABLE OF CONTENTS

Preface 1

Introduction 5

Chapter 1   The Great Analogy of Monopoly 11

Chapter 2   The Great Lie, a Slice of Pie 17

Chapter 3   Eternity vs. The Vapor 25

Chapter 4   Distractions, Distractions, Distractions 29

Chapter 5   We Are So BLESSED!
                  (Wealth and the Vapor-Minded Christian) 39

Chapter 6   Why Me? Life, Death, and Stages
                  Within the Vapor 53

Chapter 7   Seeing the Vapor for What It Is 63

Chapter 8   Getting the Vapor Right 73

Chapter 9   Yes, Enjoy the Vapor 85

Chapter 10   The Vapor is Important, Significant,
                  and Has a Purpose 97

Chapter 11   God Willing 105

Chapter 12   The Battle Goes On (yes, for me too) 113

About the Author 123

PREFACE

James 4:14 Whereas you know not what shall be tomorrow. For what is your life? It is but a vapor, which appears for a little time, then vanishes away.

What do we really believe?

WARNING (ACHTUNG) Please carefully consider what I say in this paragraph. Once you read this, you are responsible for the knowledge you have. This is your Matrix red pill or blue pill moment. Choose the blue pill, you put the book down now, and believe whatever you choose. Choose the red pill, keep reading—but prepare to raise questions, stretch your faith, and challenge your view of life as we know it.

I won't dwell long on the creation vs. evolution concept. I briefly address the basis of your belief system. What do you believe? What is the source of all the incredible, technical design of our planet—the correct balance of oxygen, carbon dioxide, nitrogen in the air, the atmosphere, the ozone layer, the sun placed at the perfect, life-sustaining 93 million miles

THE VAPOR

away from the earth? Think carefully of the high level design behind cells in all animals: the precise, harmonious bodily systems (most of which operate below our conscious thinking) breathing, heart beat, blood circulation, and so many more; the incredible sophistication behind human DNA; the awesome and mysterious organ named the human brain—the source of emotions, feelings, and thoughts, our very soul, the essence of who we are.

Do you believe the Big Bang Theory? Not many do anymore, even many scientists at least lean toward intelligent design. No disrespect, I insult no one's intelligence, but let's just be real. I'm sure we'd all agree a big explosion couldn't create all of the above, any more than a rubber factory and a metal factory could blow up next to one another resulting in a Lexus.

Do you believe there's just something/someone up there somewhere? If so, what's the purpose of it all? Come on, don't just dismiss it, *think*. Let's suppose I convince you to consider God exists, or you already accept this truth. So what is His purpose for this life? Is it reasonable to believe you are here for a specific and unique purpose that you are equipped to fulfill? Sure beats the cop-out explanation of all of this being random coincidence that began at some point.

We don't fully understand time and space continuum no matter how hard we try. Scientists have the audacity to estimate

PREFACE

the size and age of the universe! OK, it's 50 bazillion miles wide, but when you reach the so-called "end," what's on the other side?

This will really bake your noodle: A pinhead is made up of trillions of atoms each so small, a million would be invisible to the naked eye. To something far larger, the earth is atom-sized. If you've seen the movie "Men in Black," there was a cat wearing a special collar with a charm that held several galaxies. That's sort of what I'm pointing to.

The universe as we know it, is a part of a bazillion universes that make up something far larger. And that far larger thing is atom-sized to something yet larger, and so on. Conversely, atoms are made up of electrons, protons, and neutrons. We say the smallest particle is an electron. Perhaps the smallest to us. To something (perhaps even something alive), an electron is the size of our universe. And that smaller something is universe-sized to something else even smaller, and so on.

Our finite minds can neither grasp the fact that there is no beginning or end of time. Should we claim there is a beginning, what was going on a week before? What will be happening a week after the end? You get the point. God is bigger than all of what I described. Let's see your fancy-pants scientists explain all of that away with all of their equations and algorithms. God was here before any of it, and will be here after whatever you say

THE VAPOR

"after is." Stop trying to wrap your mind around it, a headache is the only likely result. And yes, bazillion is a made-up number.

How much more complex is our God who is, always was, always will be, and all-knowing of everything simultaneously? He knows how many hairs are on your head (in my case, I know that answer too—zero). He knows the thoughts, anxieties, wishes, hang-ups, histories, pasts, futures, and *everything else* about 7 billion people. He knows how much the earth weighs, the exact temperature of Pluto, and anything else you can think of. He knows what you're thinking right now.

Our feeble, finite minds far fall short of understanding. We are simply created for relationship with Him, and we're on a "need to know" basis. A wise man once said, "The smarter I get, the more I realize I don't know." As we grow in faith and understanding, it becomes clear there is so much more.

Join me on this journey, as I aim to not necessarily answer all your questions, but more so cause a shift in your heart and perhaps raise more questions in your mind. Ultimately, I pray you'll seek a deeper understanding of God, your relationship with Him, and His purpose for your life on earth. Despite your perception of the James 4:14 "vapor" we call "life," relationship with God is of utmost importance—above all that we consider high priority.

INTRODUCTION

James 4:14 Whereas you know not what shall be tomorrow. For what is your life? It is but a vapor, which appears for a little time, then vanishes away.

Honestly, I feel this scripture is one of the most important and overlooked aspects of walking out victorious Christian lives. There are others that reference the same point, but the author makes the point so directly and candidly. It's a huge key in understanding the meaning of our earthly lives. We are each entrusted with a life from God, planned before the formation of the earth. He predestined us to walk in His calling for our earthly lives. That calling glorifies God, causes us to love our brother, and draw others not walking in their calling to find their way.

Before we venture into the scripture further, I feel it is important to briefly discuss the book of James to properly set up the foundation of this important scripture. The book is an epistle (letter) which is generally considered not to be specifically

THE VAPOR

between two parties (author and subject). Rather, it seems more of a letter of instruction and guidance meant for circulation.

The argument concerning authorship of the book rages on (as with other books of the Bible). The writer simply calls himself "James, servant of God and the Lord Jesus Christ." Jesus had two apostles named James. One was the son of Zebedee, the other was the son of Alpheus. There are arguments that each of these men could have authored the book, as well as evidences that they could not have.

There can be cases made for timing, nature of the authors, language, and several other factors. There are further arguments that cite different authors altogether. While I do not discount the importance of historical data, for sake of argument, I am going to simply accept the letter as God's word sent through his messenger named James, intended to strengthen our walk with Christ.

James 4:14 states this life is but a vapor that appears for a little time then vanishes. We have all of these sayings: "Life is short," "Live for today," "Treat every day like it's your last," or "Y.O.L.O." (You only live once). The reality is that life on earth is very short, especially in comparison with eternity. We have bought into the "live for today" thinking.

My aim is to challenge us, yourself, and myself to shift our thinking. We spend the vast majority of our time in majoring in

INTRODUCTION

the minor. In other words, the short-term thinking of chasing the vapor rather than eternity.

So who am I to be writing this book? I kind of wondered that, as God downloaded this concept into my spirit. I don't have the résumé that says I should be writing such a book. Let me share a bit about myself and how it perhaps relates to this concept. I am the product of a single-parent home. My mother and father divorced when my brother and I were very young. We grew up in the rougher part of the south side of Seattle, and my mother worked two jobs most of the time just to make ends meet. I was a total latchkey kid from the time I started first grade.

From my viewpoint, I struck a pretty good balance considering the circumstances. As a family we had our ups and downs. At times there was no food in our kitchen. We've had power, phone, and other basic services shut off. We moved around a lot, much of it was not by choice. Many of the places we lived at weren't the nicest. At times, we lived in very undesirable conditions of safety and sanitation. I'm not sure which was worse—the living conditions or the impoverished, desperate mindset of some of the people around us.

There were a few times, for varying reasons, we struggled to keep a roof over our heads. We lived with relatives, with friends, stayed in missions and battered women's shelters. There were times when we simply had nowhere to go. Nonetheless, we still made the best we could with what we had. Since those days, we've come a long way. Despite our share of challenging times, I still managed to be an honor student up until my freshman year in high school. I had met and connected with Grammy-winning recording artist Sir-Mix-A-Lot and music began to absorb a large portion of my time. We traveled extensively, and my grades started to slip badly.

That all changed in a meeting with my high school counselor at the beginning of my sophomore year. He pulled my prior academic records and called me into his office. The meeting was brief and to the point. He knew I was smart and he saw me letting my opportunity slip away. He gave me the choice of being someone with a future or being a bum. I decided against being a bum, and left his office changed—just like that.

I earned a 3.83 GPA in my next semester, and despite increased traveling, I never fell under a 3.5 throughout the rest of high school. I had my mind made up that I was going to college to be an engineer. I loved math and science. By the time I was a senior in high school, I was taking honors Calculus, and was accepted into the University of Washington. My solo music career began to blossom, and my educational aspirations began to fizzle. By the time I was 19, I had a quarter million dollar house, a Mercedes, Jeep, a few bucks in the bank. Compared to where I'd come from, I thought I was rich and had it made in the shade.

INTRODUCTION

I had a pretty fascinating ride in my late teens and early 20s as a hip hop recording artist in the music business. During my run as "Kid Sensation," I sold over 1 million units, went on major tours, hung out with star athletes, entertainers, and lived what I thought to be "the dream." It was a roller coaster, to say the least. I will spare most of the details for my future autobiography. You can "google" me by name and my prior handle, "Kid Sensation." Much of my life story has been documented.

I thought my journey through the music biz was in preparation for a bigger music and entertainment career. But the next "go round" was going to be as a Christian, so it would be for a higher purpose than my own glory. I believe that may be true, but I believe it is only a portion of the story. I know there is more to it. As crazy as it sounds, I believe I was intended to write this book and that my experiences in part were designed to show me how fleeting are the things of this world.

I believe I needed to experience firsthand the quest and thirst for the tasty, good life many of us scramble for. My children were intended to be here to bring forth other attributes in me such as patience, selfless love, commitment, dedication, and patience. Yes, I know I said "patience" twice, it was intentional. If you are not a parent, once you become one, you'll quickly understand. I needed a transition period to reexamine my life, its priorities, and purpose. Somehow, I believe it all rolled into this book you are reading.

THE VAPOR

I don't have all of the qualifications that perhaps the author of this sort of book should have. I come from a broken family, none of whom had Christian backgrounds. My father isn't some big-time pastor. I don't have any bible degrees or preaching background, literary background, never taught, not an expert in any related field.

I don't know how this book will be received. I bet experts will pick it apart. I imagine there will be no shortage of critics to poke holes in it. It is really OK with me. What gives me the confidence in writing this book is the calling I firmly believe I heard to write it. Historically, from the biblical times till now, when an individual felt a calling to come forth with something they deemed important, life altering, or God-inspired, there was no shortage of opposition.

I don't have all the qualifications. In fact, I'm not sure I have any. What I do have is a faith that God doesn't necessarily call the qualified, but He most certainly qualifies the called. I'm not going to pretend one day the clouds parted and I heard some audible voice call from heaven. No chariot showed up to my house with trumpets to deliver a golden pen and pad. It was what I consider to be a meeting spurned by a series of events. I don't, however, believe it was a coincidence. Read with an open mind and heart. I am confident you will gain something out of this book.

CHAPTER 1

The Great Analogy of Monopoly

I was sitting in a coffee shop in Seattle (imagine that), talking to John Sekijama, a wonderful and wise mentor in my life. He was a huge inspiration in my writing this book. John and I met when I shared music at an outreach event put on by a mutual friend. His father had recently passed away. He told me the story of his father's life, describing him as a brilliant man who spent most of his life outside of a relationship with God. Ultimately, before his passing, his grandson (John's son) led him to a relationship with Christ. John also shared an interesting story of what he considered to be some of his father's greatest words. "Life is sort of like a game of Monopoly," John's father told him. He went on to describe how we start out, going around the board in circles, trying to get all the money and good property we can.

Anyone who's played Monopoly learns to covet Park Place, Boardwalk, even the green and yellow groups. We do a few

THE VAPOR

laps, land on a few properties, buy, sell, pull a few chance and community chest cards. The game gets competitive, trade talks heat up, we get locked in and *are determined* to win. Things can turn quickly for better or worse with just a few rolls of the dice. A few good breaks for you, some bad breaks for me, and you end up with all the best properties. Someone else sold you the railroads before they quit, giving you all four (at $200 rent, I seem to find 'em with each roll). You have houses, hotels, and so many gold $500 bills, you can use them to fan your smug little face.

I have nothing left but a few ones, fives, and I'm staring at the back of Baltic, St. Charles (because I've mortgaged them away). Then the unthinkable happens—I land on Boardwalk *with* a hotel, that's like $2,000. You offer to loan me some money or give me a pass so you can continue your reign of rule for a couple more ill-fated rolls. But I wave the white flag, and it's a wrap.

Can I sidetrack into "center field" for just a moment (pun completely intended)? This gives me vivid flashbacks of playing with a buddy of mine, Hall of Fame baseball player Ken Griffey Jr.—the fiercest Monopoly player I've met. Ken is so competitive that we have literally put "all-nighters" into games of Monopoly. We can be five hours in, the game can be OVER, he can own the whole board, have so much money—still, he has to pull money from another game box. When everyone else was

THE GREAT ANALOGY OF MONOPOLY

completely broke, it didn't matter. He wanted to keep playing. It's like that hapless mouse in the mouth of the cat, before the kill he plays with it for a while, and carries on the torture. When Ken reads this he'll chuckle, he knows it's true.

Apologies, I find that story humorous yet mildly concerning, I digress ...

You look over your great accomplishment. You have it *all*. The money, the best properties, the houses, the hotels, even the respect and envy of the others sitting around the table. You have it *all*. You lean back in your chair, count your money, and with a deep sigh you relish your win. It feels so good—it's oh, so satisfying. You started from little like we all did, and when the smoke cleared, you stood on top. OK, *now what?* That's not a rhetorical question, really *now what?* You've got it all—the power, fame, respect, *everything* you wanted in the beginning. You put in your five hours, all of your effort, attention, you worked so hard for this victory, and now *you've got it.* **Now what?**

You got it: *The game is over.* The pieces go back in the box. We spend our lives on earth like we're playing Monopoly. We run in circles doing everything to grab as much as possible to "perfect the vapor." We want the education, money, cars, and the comfortable, cushy life. We covet the 401k, the great portfolio,

THE VAPOR

the travel, the house, and the 2.5 kids. We want everything in the vapor to be just right, as close to perfect as we can get it. Then, we've arrived. We will get the peace we're searching for once we get Park Place and Boardwalk with the hotels.

According to the old saying, "Money is the root of evil." I respectfully disagree. Money is inanimate, it comes down to the *motive* or *nature* of the person behind the money. We go awry in the prioritization of *the pursuit of money over everything else.* Understand, the misdirected pursuit of money isn't just reserved for the "rich getting richer." People that struggle financially, work two or more jobs, sometimes work just as long, hard, and vapor-mindedly as the upper class.

The pursuit of money ranges from some looking to "just get ahead," to others with an insatiable quest to stockpile more than they can spend in a thousand lifetimes. Both are equally "off target" when the focus is the vapor, regardless if we have Baltic Avenue or Boardwalk (with hotel) aspirations. When it's over ... *ashes to ashes, dust to dust, pieces in box.*

In the interim, we scratch and claw for it, cry for it, lose sleep for it, go to war for it, we gotta have that sweet vapor. We get to the end of the 100 or so years of earthly life, and guess what? Everything we worked SO hard for: all we've earned, our storehouses full of grain, trust funds, bank accounts, fancy homes, and assets we neglected our relationships for, all of

THE GREAT ANALOGY OF MONOPOLY

our trinkets we held so tightly to—we take *none of it* with us. We put the pieces, *every single one*, back in the box. The vapor of this life dissipates, and we leave it all behind, no exceptions. Both the king and the servant leave *all* behind, and put *every piece* back in the box.

THE VAPOR

CHAPTER 2

The Great Lie, a Slice of Pie

My first pastor, Reggie C. Witherspoon, frequently said, "The biggest whammy our spiritual enemy pulled was to convince many of us to doubt or disbelieve in his existence." I tend to agree, as many people don't even realize they are in a spiritual battle. Thoughts, doubts, temptations, insecurities, and insignificance we face on a daily basis are part of this fight. In battle, we are at a distinct disadvantage when we are unarmed and unprotected. It's a "whole nutha level" when we are completely unaware a battle is going on.

Another key trick that has flown greatly under the radar was to get our primary focus away from eternal things, and on the vapor. It happens in a very subtle fashion. *We are conditioned to treat the vapor with priority over the eternal.* We think of the vapor as the most important part of our journey. We see a pleasure-filled vapor as our blessing and promised land. Truthfully, many of us see our earthly financial status as God's promise being fulfilled. Even lifelong, well-meaning Christians perpetuate the great lie. We get so locked into chasing the material-focused, easy, comfortable vapor that comes and goes in a blink, that we almost completely lose sight of eternity.

What were Jesus' two great commands to us in Mark 12:29–31? *Love God with all our heart, mind, soul, strength; love our neighbor as ourselves.* I've not seen it recorded where Jesus taught us principles of possessions and pleasure which we seek to spread and define as victorious life. Jesus didn't die for us to pile up money, party while we're young, and then become "religious" when we get old. He certainly didn't die to excuse us for undisciplined, mismanaged lives.

We start our lives as babies, incapable of consciously giving, so we exclusively receive. We grow, then gradually as we become adults, we learn the power of giving, and putting others first. This is exemplified when we have children. The same holds true for the most part in our spiritual walk. As we grow, our mindset should shift from selfish to selfless. We should allocate our resources prayerfully, with great wisdom and care. We should certainly understand the reality of our resources being finite. We hold on to money, possessions, and our time so tightly, but they are simply part of the vapor (which is here for an instant, then gone).

THE GREAT LIE, A SLICE OF PIE

Jesus did not instruct us to view or treat the vapor as irrelevant. It is actually very important, but along with its related contents must be kept in the correct perspective. We should carefully examine the way in which Jesus spent His time in the vapor, versus the way in which we spend ours.

We are supposed to model Him, yet He sought and taught us to serve and give. We tend to seek to be served and receive. When Jesus prayed, it was in the interest of doing the will of His Father. When we pray, it tends to be in the interest of The Father doing our will.

I have yet to find it recorded where Jesus operated like a genie to present a new chariot or house to someone. What He gave of Himself were eternal gifts, showing great compassion for humanity. His miracles build our faith to bear witness and present the opportunity for all to believe, then follow.

God's power and love were demonstrated through Jesus as He healed, taught, delivered, blessed, saved, and loved humanity. Perfect love flowed from Jesus. He was aligned with God's perfect will. His prayer the night before His crucifixion is the only one I've seen recorded, where Jesus prayed related to sparing Himself any worldly discomfort, inconvenience, or hardship. Even that prayer ended in His agreement to the will of the Father. His life ended in a brief, but profoundly impactful 33 years here on Earth.

THE VAPOR

Ask a Christian about their priorities. We all say, "God comes first in my life." We say, "God is the most important." Really? Let's put it in park there for a second. Truth be told, many of us spend 99.9% of our lives caught up chasing the vapor. We have God in us and with us, a loving, all-knowing Father with our best interests at heart. Yet, we seldom seek His wisdom or approval in our lives.

God is the same yesterday, today, and tomorrow—pure Love. He defines love in a deeper fashion than our hearts and minds can process. God isn't impulsive or moody. He doesn't change or abandon us when we err in our ways. Yet, we seek the counsel, approval, and company of people who ... well, let's just say they're people who are flawed, frail, and limited in knowledge, love, and grace.

Many of us have great hearts, mean well, and believe we truly love God. But our hearts are slightly out-of-whack, not quite dialed in. Think of a compass that's off by two degrees. It doesn't sound like much, till you follow it for a few miles. Just one degree off will land you in a completely different destination.

How far are we dialed out from God's direction, plan, protection, and relationship? We say "God first," but do we put Him behind a myriad of other things? Is our relationship with Him virtually nonexistent? Broken down to a stale routine of systematic prayer, church, and other rituals with little of our

THE GREAT LIE, A SLICE OF PIE

creativity and effort? Our time is spent on chasing and improving the vapor. Hey—we gotta live, work, and eat, right? We bring the family to church, pay tithes, even give an offering, and we don't do any of the "big, bad stuff." We have our "little" vices, but "God knows our hearts."

We've got this thing down pat. Our mouths say, "We're frail, we trust and need God, and we're not perfect." Under the surface, deep in our hearts, many of us have become our own little gods. We follow the "12 Steps to a Perfect Christian Life and Go to Heaven Plan." Do we truly lead sacrificial lives that honor God, edify others, and seek the lost? Are our hearts and motives pure, or do we have other self-serving, hidden agendas such as recognition or notoriety?

I recall my early Christian days and writing a list of all the things I had planned for my life. I knew exactly how God needed to bless me. I knew I had a gift and I was all ready for Him to use it for my plan. I almost felt as if I was some sort of highly-touted free agent, and I'd done God a favor by joining His team. I felt as long as I went to church and went through my motions of tithing, serving, occasionally invited a guest, witnessed a little here and there—I'd done my part.

I figured I was living the dream, even in a position to be a bit condescending to others since I'd "arrived." Now I figured it was time for God to pony up on His promise. It was time for the "presto magic stuff" I heard about: miracles falling out of the sky, everything in life falling into place so the world could recognize me in all my glory. My vapor was destined to be the greatest, and heaven was simply my parking place in paradise when it was all over.

We're high on the vapor, and this world system has one prince. He whispers to us, "You, my friend, are the stuff! You have it all together. You drip with Awesome Sauce!" (a saying borrowed from the great Pastor Steven Furtick). We end up becoming a bit cocky, complacent, and ineffective. Our lips say "Jesus is our Lord and Savior" just like our lips say "God is first," but our lives seem to differ. We give Jesus our "all," but we hold back certain things. Some things we can trust God with, but not with everything. Certain parts we tell ourselves "I've got this" and we decide to handle it our way.

At a certain point, we feel we've "arrived," as our vapor is exactly what society and everyone else deems successful. We have now become "vapor-accomplished," earning the approval and admiration of man. This becomes a tricky spot. We soon become dependent upon our plan (that coincidentally fits neatly into our own desires) rather than God's plan. Our lives look how we envisioned them, but are they structured and destined the way in which God intended?

Let's look at our lives like a pie, sliced 24 times to represent 24 hours in a day. How many slices of that pie do we spend

THE GREAT LIE, A SLICE OF PIE

working? Shuffling to and fro? Texting? Locked in on the latest gadget or widget, and then learning how to use it? In fellowship, hanging out with the peoples? Surfing the net? Sleeping, eating, and taking care of the flesh body to get it "just right"? Pursuing hobbies? Watching TV? After adding up all our activity, how much of that pie is left for God?

There's nothing wrong with all that stuff, when kept in correct perspective. We have to keep a balance, and here is the kicker: we should include God in EVERY piece of that pie. That is correct—God should be a part of EVERY slice. We should consider God's will and purpose in all we do.

This is not to say we shouldn't enjoy carefree moments. Relaxation time, refreshment time, vacations, mindless TV time, laying in a hammock "do nothing" time are for most of us integral parts of life. Pleasure moments are equally important to our lives as work, but not necessarily of equal proportion. The key is, all of our moments, even our pleasures, should tie into God's plan for us. He will guide us on the proper balance.

Include God in *every* slice of our pie, and sprinkle the entire pie with *eternal flavor*. When I say "eternal flavor," I mean look at *everything*—big and small. Factor God into the equation and measure all we consider—based upon *eternity*,

THE VAPOR

not the 100 or so years we plan to live on earth. It gave me a new perspective on the vapor and helped me to comprehend the vapor's real purpose. God wants relationship with us. He gave us the power to choose relationship with Him.

In Mark 12:29-31, Jesus tells us it's most important to love the Lord our God with all our heart, soul, mind, and strength. We are to also love one another as ourselves. Jesus stated there is no command greater than these. Jeremiah 29:11 says the Lord has great plans for you. He wants you to prosper in life, be filled with hope and have a great future. These are very familiar passages of scripture to many.

I know you get it, but do you *really* get it?

CHAPTER 3

Eternity vs. The Vapor

When we think about time in the finite, we as people consider the timeline of the vapor almost exclusively. Time is one of those awesome mysteries surrounding God. How can God or time "always have been" or "always be"? When we have to wait 30 minutes in a line at the post office, we say "Wow, that took forever!" We sigh at the concept of it taking "all day" to help someone move to a new house or to serve others. When expecting God to move on our behalf, we may give up if we don't see results in a day, a month, or year. "Come on, that's just way too long!"

Let's examine our lives versus eternity. I'd say most of us feel like 100 years is a long, long time. Just think to yourself of 10 or even 20 years ago, and how long it seems. Our finite minds cannot truly comprehend infinite things. Here's an illustration. Let's say a bird is standing on the beach in Venice, California. This bird grabs one grain of sand, and flies it from Venice to

≡VAPOR

Maui, Hawaii (yes, it's 2,500 miles and physically impossible). Don't get technical, just go with me. He drops off the grain of sand and then flies back to Venice Beach. The bird continues this process, grain by grain, to move sand from Venice to Maui. When the bird has successfully moved the trillions and trillions of grains of sand that comprise the entire Venice Beach over the 2,500 miles to Maui, eternity has just begun. Wow. Do those 100 years seem as long anymore?

They say our sun will last another five billion years before it burns out and turns into a white dwarf. Five billion years is but a blink in comparison to eternity. So if our life on earth is 100 years and eternity follows, why do we spend such a large percentage of our focus on the initial 100 years?

If I told you I was going to shorten your life by one tenth of one second, would you panic? Probably not. In the linear, human perception of time, we have roughly 100 years give or take. So a tenth of a second is pretty insignificant. If you were 25 years old and I said I would shorten your life by 70 years, would this change your perspective? Now, not only would most of us panic—but all of a sudden, even a year becomes a short time.

Isn't it ironic? When expecting God to move on your behalf, a year seems "forever." It's not really ironic, it's actually quite simple. We think and live in a very finite, linear manner with

ETERNITY vs. THE VAPOR

our 100 year timeline. We base our considerations of time upon the world system (and we know the prince of that system). This skews our perspective of reality and big picture, eternal-minded thinking.

Eternal-thinking contradicts vapor-minded thinking. Since eternal things cannot change, we change our perception of eternal things to fit our vapor "reality." Moreover, our perception of reality is defined by vapor-minded concepts and people. Most of us don't get it, and we tend to misunderstand, or be in awe of those who do.

We attempt to use finite, vapor-minded concepts to define and understand eternal things.

I saw on TV, the story of a little girl dying from cancer. She was given just a few months to live. The piano slowly played while they talked about her sad story. They gave the details of her condition, remarked at the hopelessness, and questioned how a vibrant life was ending so young. But when she spoke, the tale she told was very different. She and her family happened to be Christian. They'd accepted her condition, and most certainly prayed repeatedly for her healing. But as her days progressed, they understood it, she got it.

God doesn't heal or cure everyone we ask Him to. However, God's promise of heaven is real, and they seemed to understand that the life here was but a vapor—this little young lady

THE VAPOR

was preparing for eternal things. Rather than shrinking back, she actually became bolder. She was determined to use the remaining days of her life in a manner that showed great appreciation and perspective of the vapor. There was such a peace about her. She had no fear of death as she knew the eternal gift of heaven, peace, and the embrace of God forever was to follow.

So why do babies die? Why do some people recover when we pray for them and others don't? Why do some seem to get a "raw deal" in their life on earth with their circumstances, their surroundings? Only God can answer why the vapor for some is one minute, a year, a decade, or a century. But in the perspective of a God to whom a billion years is a blink, He sees infinitely more than our finite minds see. The real question is: *What are we going to do with our time here?* Will we spend it chasing the perfect vapor for ourselves and others, or on eternal things?

CHAPTER 4

Distractions, Distractions, Distractions

So what got us here? How did we all get so caught up, so dialed in to the vapor? One factor has been key: *Distractions*. The distractions of the vapor are complex system of thoughts, people, actions, and activities that occupy our minds.

In some cases, distractions come disguised as "innocent stuff" everyone thinks, says, or does. In other instances they may be perhaps legal but immoral. In other cases altogether, they may be socially unacceptable or illegal. Distractions range from relationships, to habits, guilty pleasures, vices, and strongholds. They also include media, sports, the Internet blogs, fantasy football, and coveting the American dream, drinking, smoking, partying, taking drugs, sex, gambling, and so much more. Think of the effects of division amongst people—from racism, classism, and religion. The list of vapor-based distractions is almost endless.

THE VAPOR

Some distractions aren't necessarily bad for us. I certainly enjoy a good movie, sporting event, concert, book, or vacations. God wired us to want pleasure and relaxation time. It's OK to enjoy ourselves. I plan to address this further a bit later in the book. The key here is that we must learn God's truth for ourselves and make daily, hourly, minute-by-minute decisions on whether or not we are too distracted.

Prayerfully consider your life. Think over relationships, activities, developing in your purpose, and how you spend the pie we discussed. Are your distractions in good proportion with the other areas of your life? Do they interfere with your purpose? Do they lead you to vapor-minded thinking? Or do they hinder your relationships with people or most importantly, God?

Consider conducting a life inventory to see if your distractions skew your focus further into vapor.

We are alive for a purpose. We have been fearfully and wonderfully made. Think of the tremendous investment that God made in you. God designed you perfectly atom by atom, cell by cell, from your DNA to your personality, gifts, talents, and abilities. Think back of the time we've wasted being distracted in our lives. When we are distracted, it's like taking a detour away from our purpose for our lives. If we start at point A, and are headed in our God-given destiny for

DISTRACTIONS, DISTRACTIONS, DISTRACTIONS

our lives at point B, the shortest distance is a straight line. Let's keep it 100 percent real. No one's line is completely straight. We all take detours on this path and make choices that affect the path, but the hope is that we find our way back to the path. A detour can be a minute or several decades, and it can be a small speed bump or a trip over a cliff, theoretically speaking. Single or multiple distractions can cause us to lose the focus on our real God-given purpose.

How about technology? Technology is fantastic. A game changer, it contributes to us accomplishing more and living better. But it can also serve as a gateway to getting lost in the vapor. Technology is a good thing. Issues arise when we get distracted or lost in the maze of technology, to the degree it completely takes us off path to our purpose. Technology is advancing over 100 times faster than it was 100 years ago and increasing exponentially. The accomplishments of our forefathers were truly incredible, but most inventions took years to develop, refine, and become a part of mainstream society.

Compare them to today's advances—we get new inventions shoved into our faces over every thinkable medium at an incredible rate. No one can keep up with all of it. It seems once we buy or download the latest gadget, get it home and unwrap it, something more advanced has been unveiled. To date, more than 500,000 applications are available for

THE VAPOR

smart phones and that number is rapidly increasing. I don't know if there were even 500,000 total man-made inventions prior to the 20th century. It's enough to make our heads spin.

Technology is a huge portal for our spiral into vapor-minded thinking. I cannot overemphasize the fact that technology is awesome and serves many great purposes. However, *we connect to God in stillness and silence.* Psalm 46:10 reads: *Be still and know that I am God.*

We seldom spend time being still or silent. We are always in the presence of people, the constant chatter of our radios, televisions, and computers. They distract us from the still and silent state in which we encounter God's presence. If we get caught away from them, we grab an iPod and shove the ear buds into our ears. We feel like we somehow need the reassurance of sounds, music, human voices whether in person, or through broadcast mediums to fill the heaviness of simple still and silence.

Ever try going to sleep and you simply cannot shut down the thoughts racing through your mind? Can you fall asleep without TV or music? We make excuses and shuffle off every opportunity to be still and silent. Many of us are afraid to face the still silence because we are running from who we are called to be.

DISTRACTIONS, DISTRACTIONS, DISTRACTIONS

The presence of God forces us to recognize and reconcile with the very borders of our flesh and spirit.

Radio and TV started out with only a few stations. Most families owned one or no TV. Over the decades, radio and TV evolved, added cable, movies, and so many options. Both served as platforms to get information, entertainment, and messages across to the masses. They now come in so many forms, and much of the content is completely unchecked. There are few requirements to broadcast, a lack of quality control, and virtually no structure filtering out spun opinion or flat-out lies. They have become a means of control over many, a way to keep the masses focused on the vapor.

Most people receive what is broadcasted as truth. We see a real news anchor, very official-looking desk and background. They speak properly and come from a big network. We seldom attempt to qualify what we're told, and most that qualify it do so from a vapor-minded perspective. We must take what is told to us and hold it up to the light of truth. Lies, whether blatant or subtle, are still lies. Stay with me, I promise I'm on topic and plan to bring this thought full circle.

Some people get so wrapped up in soap operas and fictitious shows, that in some cases, they create a false reality around them. Many soap stars playing the roles of villains have gotten actual death threats from viewers disgruntled with their character's actions. There are soap opera magazines and shows to update us on the latest details and rumors about fictitious characters. For those that need more, there's "reality" TV—canned, staged, rehearsed shows we're compelled to watch that sensationalize the episodes of others' lives.

We follow celebrities dancing, people disclosing a big secret, going to court, cooking, eating, losing weight, catching fish, catching crooks, partying, driving, crashing, dating, getting married, swapping wives, getting divorced, spoiled kids' birthday parties. And if that wasn't enough, we had to "keep up" with one family that seems to have all of the above going on.

If this isn't enough, we have channels (that's right), entire channels dedicated to 24 hours of just about any subject we can imagine. I'd imagine the people who were around when there were only three channels could never imagine there would be entire networks dedicated to cars, houses, cooking, comedy, fishing, poker, "adult" (pornographic) and so much more. There are channels many of us would consider quite ridiculous, but if there were no demand, the channel would likely not exist. It seems to be a blatant attempt at creating a revenue-generating distraction for every imaginable human desire.

Let's factor in the commercials that are currently broadcasted. They tell us what we should want to eat, where to live, how to live, how we want to look, feel, and think. "Come on! Eat this

DISTRACTIONS, DISTRACTIONS, DISTRACTIONS

tasty, preservative-packed, unhealthy food in huge servings. Super-size me, go BIG, we're American. Here's antacid to mask the heartburn." "Now, we're obese and suffering severe health conditions? No problem, we have weight-loss products, appetite suppressants, drugs, fad diets, even a TV show where contestants compete to lose weight and deprogram all they've been sold." "Drink alcohol, great times are found with friends and liquor. Are you now an alcoholic? Come to our new place for our 12-day, 12-step process to get your life back."

Have you seen the drug company commercials? Wow. They have a new condition for *everything*. "Does your back itch? You may be suffering from itchy-back syndrome. Ask your doctor about 'Youbegone' to treat symptoms of an itchy back. Side effects can range from mild to severe, including skin rash, headaches, dizziness, irregular heartbeat, coma, death, nosebleed while standing or sitting, and you could go on a bank robbery spree. Don't take 'Youbegone' if you live near a bank, own a gun, or plan to sit down later." You get the point.

The common denominator in the vast majority of commercials broadcasted is they seek to sell us pleasure, pain, the remedy for the pain, then more pleasure. They make their pleasure seem so enticing, so irresistible that we have to have it. We've gotta buy new car, take that vacation. I mean hey, what happens in Vegas stays in Vegas—how can you turn that down? It all seems so good. "Oh man, we're going to get so much pleasure behind the wheel

THE VAPOR

of our shiny automobile, sipping that tasty latté, in that great outfit. People are going to see us—and oh man, they are going to be so impressed! *Ahh, it will be so gratifying!"* We get caught up—*really, really caught up*—because we're trying to satisfy a thirst that cannot be quenched.

The system we live in is designed to keep us distracted and seeking a pleasure-filled vapor. Its very structure can eventually lead us to miss the mark for our eternity.

Computers. Oy, computers have been around for 80 years. The first "supercomputer" took up an entire floor of a building, and handled a mind-blowing number of calculations per second. Well, mind-blowing for that era. Fast forward to today. Your smart phone is far more powerful, in the palm of your hand. Think for a moment how so much has changed so rapidly. We can video chat, pay for a latté, communicate with hundreds or millions of people instantly through social networking. We can "google" anything under the sun and get instant information, whether from a desktop, laptop, or right from our phones.

Unfortunately, computers have created another huge gateway to being distracted and vapor-minded. We spend hours on websites, social media sites, blogs. Our home page is riddled with interesting stories about people, links to articles

DISTRACTIONS, DISTRACTIONS, DISTRACTIONS

and videos with sensational titles so we are drawn to check them out. We search for entertainment, love, plane tickets.

And don't fool around and get caught up on YouTube. People broadcast themselves saying and doing just about anything to the entire world. Once you've watched a video, there are scores of other related videos in the cue—all with juicy, compelling titles just waiting for you to click and watch. Online gaming has completely blown up. We can play video games against real people all around the world in real time. The billions of pages and websites online are enough to keep anyone distracted for twenty lifetimes.

Clearly, computers are not all bad, nor is the Internet. I completed a ton of my research for this book on the Internet. I searched for quotes, data, and relative scriptures. I typed every word of this book on my laptop. The issue isn't whether or not the computer and Internet are bad. Like a knife, it depends on what you use a computer for. And like a knife not handled properly, it can present real danger.

So many distractions. We've only begun to scratch the surface. Here's the key. If your enemy can keep you distracted, it causes you to be less effective. Being distracted can keep us from realizing we're in a battle. It can lull us to sleep, and leave us vulnerable to being sucker-punched.

THE VAPOR

I felt it necessary to do an inventory of my life, my surroundings, and the influence distractions had on me. If I want to be who I'm destined to be, I've got to keep a firm handle on vapor-centered things and eternal things. If I choose to be distracted and vapor-minded, there is plenty for me to find right on my TV, computer, or radio. And I admit I enjoy watching sports, news, and an occasional show. Other than that, I watch very little TV and listen to very little radio. While I seek to fill the "lonely" silence with distractions, chatter, company, and noise, the loving voice of God's spirit whispers to me: *"In My presence is all which you seek."*

CHAPTER 5

We Are So BLESSED!

(Wealth and the Vapor-Minded Christian)

This may be a controversial statement and a tough pill to swallow for some, but are we really so sure God is concerned about us piling up money to experience all of the "creature comforts" in the vapor? Is God really focused on John Doe's house being paid off, his Lexus, timeshare in Maui, expensive suits, and jewelry?

What does that say to all the people in third world countries that have no concept of such things? They have no access to clean water. They bathe in filthy rivers with animals, waste, and in some places, our discarded computer parts (yes, it's true; research it for yourself). They have little or no food, no access to health care, scores die young or suffer lifelong trauma from curable diseases. Many suffer great physical anguish and agony, they are crippled with no wheelchairs or physical assistance. Some are victims of rape, torture, murder, theft, molestation, persecution, violence, and lawless living conditions. They cry out to God to help them out of dire, severe, and life-threatening consequences.

God instead "chooses to bless" John Doe who racked up a quarter million dollars of debt on ill-advised purchases, gives him a big fancy house and SUV that suck up more of earth's resources than 50 families elsewhere? This is merely a question I pose, and I don't claim to have all the answers. I'm certainly not saying to stop praying for God to make a way out of our poor choices. I'd say we should carefully consider our motives when we ask God to do something. I'd further venture to say we often miss the *purpose* behind finances and responsibilities that come with.

We each must examine our own hearts and the motives behind our desire for financial increase.

"Everyone check us out, we are so BLESSED! We have the perfect vapor, a big house, cars, jewelry, big bank account, and we don't have any debt. Oh, look what God did!" Listen, you are blessed, and God has done wonderful works in your life. And I do not even doubt that He opened up the windows of heaven to pour out a financial blessing for you. Be aware—be careful that your testimony isn't leading other Christians down a slippery slope of equating God's favor to the size of their bank account.

Blessing isn't measured in dollars and cents. It isn't counted by the number of earthly treasures we accumulate. All that stuff is great, but perhaps we shouldn't get so caught up

WE ARE SO BLESSED!

counting that Monopoly money lest we forget that blessing is so much more.

Be careful not to mislead yourself or others who look to your example as absolute truth. The fulfillment of God's purpose isn't centered in money. Furthermore, we serve a jealous God who is not pleased with treasures put before Him. It happens in a subtle but steady fashion where before we know it, our pie shows that money and things have become our idols, prioritized before God.

There are warnings in the Bible about financial wealth. It's not the money or the things we acquire. It's about the lust, greed, and passion for it—the feeding of our selfish desires, prioritizing wealth above relationship with God and one another. Let's make it crystal clear. The purpose of wealth is expanding God's Kingdom. I'm not stating that the acquisition and possession of wealth are bad. Nor am I stating that having stuff is an issue. The issue lies in us losing track of the purpose of wealth.

God probably examines our hearts and in His infinite wisdom and grace knows when to allow what He chooses to allow. We are to follow the example of Jesus. I have not seen it recorded in the Bible or elsewhere that Jesus worked to acquire a bunch of stuff and things for Himself.

In the Bible, Luke 12:16-34, Jesus tells a parable that seems to state otherwise. A certain rich man had a windfall of crops.

The man wonders what to do with his newfound and additional wealth. He has a vapor-minded "ah ha" moment and decides to tear down his current barns to build *bigger* ones—to store up all of his crops and goods. The man then says he can tell his soul to be at ease, eat, drink, and be merry.

Does that sound familiar? Does it seem relatively close to what we think? This chain of thought causes the man to collect himself a firm rebuke, which I saw as a verbal "Three Stooges style slap" on the back of his head. It is then recorded in Luke 12:20-21, Jesus continues: *"But God said to him, 'Fool!'* (I love this part of the parable for the lesson it teaches and also because Jesus uses the word "fool." It's always so appropriate, yet funny.) *On this night your soul shall be required of you; then whose will those things be which you have provided? He who lays treasure up for himself, is not rich toward God."* Oops.

My point from this parable continues to Luke 12:36. Jesus continues to teach us not to worry about our lives, stock up, or store up; not to be anxious or try to run after all the meaningless stuff like the world. He does tell us if we seek God's kingdom first, that these things would be added unto us. He taught us that our hearts are with our treasures. Carefully consider what He is teaching us here. *Our heart is with our treasure.*

This is not to say we can measure up to His standard, nor be perfect. What conclusion could be drawn through parables,

WE ARE SO BLESSED!

Jesus exemplified the fact that with great wealth comes great responsibility.

More stuff tends to equal more of our time, energy, and focus to maintain it.

Where is the line drawn between necessity and excess? If we desire a 10,000 square foot home—cool. The $80,000 sports car—great. The $20,000 watch—OK. But get to the root of the "why." Does our stuff further our walk with God, our testimony, and help us bring more people further into the knowledge of Christ? No? OK, if not, let's at the very least be sure it doesn't take the place of God in our lives. God won't pay as much attention to the house we owned, as He does to how many people we sheltered. Nor will He care about the type of car we drove, as much as who we gave rides to.

We have to prayerfully consider our purpose in whatever we acquire. Does the acquisition and retention of the stuff keep our relationship with God out of balance? "Seek ye first the kingdom of God and His righteousness and He will grant the desires of your heart." Oh, we love that. So if we become super Christians, super deep, He'll give us all the money, cars, clothes, travel, and all the stuff our heart desires? Sign me up! Well, I'm not sure that's exactly it. We take many of the vapor comforts for granted—health, food, shelter, etc. and allow the pursuit of "greater vapor" to take priority. This cheapens the cost at the

THE VAPOR

Cross. We actually become servants of materialism and greed, rather than servants of Jesus who loves us beyond measure.

No one can serve two masters. You will love one and hate the other, or you will hold on to one and despise the other. You cannot serve both God and money. — Matthew 6:24

When we reach the finish line of the vapor and come before God, we all strive to hear those words, "Well done, humble and faithful servant." The real issue is that wealth in some cases adds unseen complexities to the "humble and faithful" part. Many people fall into a false sense of "arrival" after attaining financial wealth in the vapor. A haughty, puffed-up spirit can strip the edge away from our hunger and passion for God.

You know how it is during "happy days," when the money is flowing well. I mean, we still give God the "credit," say how "blessed" we are, we go through all the "good Christian" motions. So maybe the prayer life loses a little edge and we don't press quite as hard for God's favor, presence, and real relationship. OK, so we don't work quite as diligently to reach unsaved people. We've lost a little of that zeal from the early days of being saved, but we drop a few extra bucks in the offerings, so that justifies our absence in other areas. Honestly, it says to God that money should give us a bit of a pass from a sacrificial commitment to our calling.

WE ARE SO BLESSED!

God opposes the proud, but shows favor to the humble.
— James 4:6

Money can make us a bit complacent, even arrogant. We erect our little castles, stock up our storehouses, then maintenance and improvement become our priority. We stand back and admire our work, just like the Monopoly game. We think we're a little more "right," a little more "blessed" than others, as we look at the "fruit" of our lives. We have money and all the vapor comforts. We have the audacity to think we can buy our way through life, our Christian walk, and into heaven. God isn't moved by our tokens. He is moved by our genuine heart to be in relationship with Him. Whatever we have and give was His to begin with.

We cannot hide our hearts or motives from God.

There is a story in the Bible, Luke 21:1-4, where the wealthy were giving gifts to the temple treasury. A poor widow approaches and gave two small coins, but they were all she had. Jesus proclaimed that this widow gave more than all of the other wealthy givers. She sacrificially gave all she had out of her poverty, while the others gave from their wealth. When we're wealthy, we feel like we've done the church, the people, and God some big favor since our gift was bigger than everyone else's. God is most concerned about the heart in our giving. Is it sacrificial? Are we giving big gifts to be seen in hopes someone will notice, and that we'll score "people points"?

THE VAPOR

Giving back to God from our earnings (also known as tithing) is a biblical part of our lives. The word "tithe" actually means 10%. Our giving should come from a place of joy.

Looking at the other side of things, vapor mentality can also prevent us from the true generosity with our finances. As a Christian, take a look at your tithing. Do you tithe 10% of your income plus give offerings?

Some people have a limited income and think they cannot give 10% because they fear they will not be able to make ends meet. Some people have a large income and don't give 10% because the amount seems overwhelming. In both cases, people begin looking at the amount of money and perhaps think of other things it could be used for. Their grip tightens on their wallet, and various thoughts come to mind: *"I'm already struggling, and they want me to give?" "If I give it to them, I will have less, they will have more." "They look like they're doing pretty well to me." " My little bit won't make a difference." "This is mine, mine, mine! I worked for it. I'll give the amount I'm comfortable with." "My gift is probably bigger than most of these other people. They should appreciate whatever I decide to give."* As my pastor Kevin Gerald would say, "The 'Me Monster' comes to life." Vapor thinking begins to take over.

The Bible states that when we tithe, our finances are blessed. When we do not, they are cursed. (Don't get all funny-faced with me, it's in the Bible. Check out Malachi 3:6-12. Any further questions are above my pay grade, you gotta take them up with God.) You gotta get in the mentality that the first 10% automatically belongs to God. Then the remainder is your new, BLESSED 100% to operate from. Here comes your $1000 check. Now you're at the fork in the road of what to do. *Read my lips:* God can do more through your $900 than you can do with your $1000. Furthermore, it often comes back in more forms than financial. Matthew 6:21 tells us where our treasure is, our heart will also be. Is your treasure in Heaven and eternal things, or in temporary earthly things?

To those who hold their pockets tight, thinking the church is out to "get your money"—with all due respect, Sir or Madam, God doesn't *"need"* you or your money. God's church will go on with or without you. The purpose of any speaker emphasizing tithing should be getting each of us in order with God's plan for our lives. Many churches around the world have ethical teams of servants seeking to do God's kingdom work. However, they are still people, and *all* people are flawed needing to be covered by God's grace. Don't let a few misguided fools who misappropriate funds ever discourage you from obedience to God's word.

Furthermore, as my friend Pastor Micahn Carter so eloquently stated, "You are willing to trust a Pastor and Church with your soul, but not your finances? That's SO stupid!" There are plenty of great resources available on tithing, offerings, and giving to

THE VAPOR

gain wisdom and understanding on the topic. In a nutshell, we are simply to give out of love, joy, and doing the will of God to expand His kingdom. We have to guard our mindset in our giving. We can sometimes be compelled, convinced, even coerced to give in order to receive—due to a materialistic, selfish, vapor mindset.

The hearts of vapor-minded Christians can be dangerous to themselves and others. They can lead us all into a "genie mentality" about God. Following a vapor-minded example, while not understanding God's love and nature, can leave us frustrated, disappointed, and hopeless. We think we can please God in all of our imperfection with a few good deeds, then cause Him to flood our bank account.

We are saved by grace, not by actions. Let's keep it simple. God wants relationship with us, for us to love on one another, and to reach the lost. When we testify of the goodness of God, is it about relationship with Him? Loving one another? Helping a lost soul find their way? Due to our perception of God's favor and blessing, it seems to default to vapor-minded stuff, most frequently money.

People want to matter, be accepted, and feel like they belong. Many people pursue money as a solution to unresolved insecurity and insignificance.

The "vapor-lack mentality" (or what vapor-minded people define as "poor") can cause similar issues. The vapor-lack mentality causes us to miss richness in spirit, health, family, love, and other life experiences. Society teaches us to be locked in on finances, material possessions, and achievements. Review your pie. What are your motives in praying for financial blessing? "Oh God, if You would just bless me with this house, car, job (you fill in the blank) that would just be soooo great. It would give me so much pleasure, security, and comfort." That's all fine, but do we then start to covet the "good life"? Do we begin to prioritize these things over relationship and dependence on God?

When you ask, you do not receive because you ask with the wrong motives—that you may spend what you get on your own pleasures. — James 4:3

We see it on TV—we hear about the celebrities, we want to taste that fame, fortune, and all that yummy, sparkly, good stuff. It starts to consume us. We start to envy those with it. We get so wrapped up, so desperate to obtain all the pleasures we feel we've been denied and watch others enjoy. Some of us even get bitter toward those we perceive to have more than we do. Mainstream media perpetuates this thinking. Christians and non-Christians alike tend to get sucked in.

Some of us believe certain people are "more blessed" than others because of the size of their bank account. I'm not so certain God has His hand in helping certain individuals accumulate massive finances. Perhaps as God gave us all gifts

THE VAPOR

and choice, some simply choose to use their gifts to increase financially. Carefully consider whether you believe that God is caught up in something so vapor-focused.

We have to search our hearts, truly search them deeply. If the windfall came tomorrow, what would your checklist look like? What would you buy first? Most would pay off the bills, buy the house, the car, go travel, and take care of all the pleasure-driven desires. Then when they got around to it, they may give a token or two to charity. Do any of the top ten items on our checklist affect our eternity or that of others?

People with the vapor-lack mentality want the money for the peace they feel it will bring them. We would buy every item on our checklists, because we feel it would bring us more peace. A big, warm home with no mortgage gives us the security and peace that we won't have to ever feel like we'll be homeless in the cold. It is also a status symbol, so that the other vapor-minded people will think highly of us. And with their approval, we have less anxiety of what others think about us, which adds more peace. Same with the new shiny car, nice clothes, and jewelry.

We want to travel so we can experience the "ahh" of relaxation. We picture ourselves in Acapulco with a backdrop similar to the beer commercial—where the guy and gal are facing the ocean in total peace, having escaped the hustle and bustle of life. We picture ourselves having to work less, taking it easy, being served a little more than we have to serve—so much peace, ahh …

But this is only vapor peace.

Let's make this clear, and I'm talking especially to Christian people. And non-Christians, you'll figure this out. The purpose of wealth is to advance the Kingdom of God. It is done with diligence, wisdom, and prudence. And we can have our "stuff" along the way. Please get this point! The "stuff" is not the issue. It's the place in our lives that the stuff takes and how much of our lives we dedicate to the acquisition, maintenance, and "protection" of our stuff.

Do we feel like we can "fool" God into thinking that we'd somehow change and become generous with a lot of money when we are selfish with a little? Do we think our present lazy lifestyles will inspire God to give us more money to bring out more of the laziness we already display? God understands our hearts and mindset. We think of all the good stuff money can bring, but we miss an important caveat: *Money can make our vapor more complex.*

Watch out! Be on guard against all forms of greed; life is not comprised of the abundance of possessions. — Luke 12:15

In Matthew 19:24, Jesus states, "Again I tell you, it is easier for a camel to go through the eye of a needle than for a rich man

THE VAPOR

to enter the kingdom of God." Simply put, when we attain financial prosperity, it's easy to get caught up in the "ahh" of the vapor. We lose sight of the pursuit of the big prize, our God-given purpose, and assignment in life.

We can spend a lifetime pursuing money, only to realize in the end that money is not what's most important.

Money only makes us more of who we are. God understands this well. You can't simply pass Ferrari keys to a person who's driven an old Buick all their life—a wreck is almost a certainty. There is a reason why lottery winners who were previously poor frequently end up broke in a few years. There is a similar reason why financially successful people can go broke and get it all back.

The trend is less of my point than the overall mindset. Wealth is not predominately about money, it is more about the mindset. Being wealthy or rich encompasses fullness of spirit, love, generosity, kindness, grace, peace, health, joy, and so much more. Money is a factor, but true wealth is not determined by the presence or absence of money. Truly wealthy people understand the many factors of wealth and the grace of God. The wealthy know material items eventually go away—all part of a vapor that precedes eternity.

CHAPTER 6

Why Me? Life, Death, and Stages Within the Vapor

Think of all the earthly suffering. In third world countries, babies starve to death and die of curable diseases, poverty, war, suffering, child trafficking, and much more. In our own country, children go hungry, there is sex trafficking, child abuse, mass shootings at schools, malls, movie theaters, and other horrific events. We wonder why bad things happen to good people, and good things happen to bad people. We find ourselves in tough situations and tend to ask God (or those who don't believe may simply pose the question), "Why Me?" "Why this tough day, tough times with turmoil, distress, family troubles, cancer, losing a job or loved ones?" Why me? I didn't do anything. I'm a pretty nice person. Why do I have to suffer or endure tough circumstances?

In the book of Job in the Bible, Job was a righteous man of great stature and wealth. He had the goods, the tangibles,

THE VAPOR

intangibles, financial wealth, possessions, family, spirit, love, and then some. As many of us know, satan claimed to God that if he had the opportunity to bring affliction and tragedy to Job's life, he felt Job would curse God. However, the Lord knew the strength and resolve of His servant Job. God allowed satan to attack Job in just about every imaginable way, short of taking his life. Health, wealth, family, and all the earthly stuff was gone.

Job questioned and went through a cycle of emotions, but remained faithful. Through a few twists and turns, we know God fully restored Job to better than before. We can all look to Job's story for comfort when we experience rough times and expect that God will restore us. *But what about people God never restores the way He did Job?*

Here is where we as Christians sometimes get foggy. When someone gets sick, we begin to pray. We fully believe they will recover from their sickness. But suppose they do not, and they die? Now, all of a sudden, we don't have answers or we clumsily throw in our insight into why God may not have "come through." Who exactly do we think we are? Everyone's vapor is not equal.

God's promise does not apply to everyone's vapor in the same manner. God's promise is an eternal gift of paradise with Him.

WHY ME? LIFE, DEATH, AND STAGES WITHIN THE VAPOR

Some people die without ever experiencing the comfortable and cushy vapor lifestyle. Some people have lives full of earthly suffering not due to their own good or bad choices. Some people are born in countries and areas where there is severe famine, poverty, social discord, war, persecution, and other atrocities. Some people live with physical ailments or sickness which cause life to be challenging in various ways. Some children are born and live a few minutes or days, months or years, and they may die prematurely. So, we defer to the canned explanation of it "being God's time." Yes, that's true, but do we truly see God's purpose behind it?

The vapor-minded see life ending, while the eternal-minded see eternity beginning and heaven rejoicing. Our earthly life no matter what the length, is a quick stage, over in a blink—intended to lead into eternity with God. When we say it's God's time, we have to complete the explanation. Yes, it's God's time, all time is His time. But let's examine a level deeper.

We may not know the specific reasons why an earthly life lasts a minute, a year, a decade, or a century. In our vapor mentality, we believe a life is too short when it doesn't fall under the guidelines of longevity we comprehend as normal—let's say 70 to 80 years. Once again, it is an example of our linear, finite minds attempting to comprehend eternal things from a vapor mindset. God created our lives (no matter how long or brief we view them) with a specific purpose and plan. The length of our lives, the ailments, the hang-ups, short-comings, circumstances, etc.—none of these trouble God in any way. We are not accidents, nor do our lives or issues therein surprise God.

I participate in charity work for women and orphaned children that are victims of violence in the DRC (Democratic Republic of Congo), Africa. Most of us have no idea of the many stories of horrific acts committed by thugs who run the lawless country. They pillage the tin, tungsten, diamonds, and gold. These precious metals are then sold to us (through various channels) in our laptops, smart phones, and shiny jewelry we covet. With a weak government structure and legal system, might makes right. These criminals rule with an iron fist and carry out their deeds ruthlessly.

The women told stories of rebels storming their villages, capturing young men and boys, then forcing them into slavery to work in mines or to fight as soldiers. Armed thugs entered villages and forced the villagers to go outside. They rounded up all of the young men and boys they wanted as workers (10 to 16-year-olds are ideal—old enough to work, but small enough to fit into very small spaces in the mines). They drugged and coerced young boys, forcing them to decide between killing or dying, in order to cultivate more rebel soldiers.

WHY ME? LIFE, DEATH, AND STAGES WITHIN THE VAPOR

No one wanted their children alongside these soldiers or working these mines, but refusal meant the public and brutal death of entire families. The mine conditions are absolutely dangerous and unregulated. When mines cave in, they become the grave of the men and children inside. They would simply cover the hole and dig another. The stories of women who lost husbands and children were numerous. Rape and murder are used as weapons of fear and coercion. In the DRC, an estimated 1200 women are raped each day; scores of people are murdered; thousands of young boys are forced to be slaves or soldiers.

Upon hearing the story of one woman, it troubled me so deeply, I'll never forget it. She was in her village when rebels came to take some young men. They went into homes and huts, rounded up everyone and brought them outside. They slaughtered several people in front of the entire village. They grouped together all of the women and began raping several of them in plain view of the other men, women, and children. They shuffled off all of the men and boys who were to be workers and soldiers.

She continued her story, sharing that the men then told her brother to have sex with her. He refused, and they cut into his head with a machete and killed him in front of her. They continued brutally raping and beating her, and the rest of the roughly 50 women present. They stabbed, cut, and shot women at random. In a fit of rage, the rebel leader elected to kill them all. At this time, one of the many men raping her discharged his rifle in her vagina. Although bleeding severely, she was able to lay in hiding among the bodies of several of the slain women. She was the only survivor.

Once the men left, she hobbled to a nearby road, clothed only in a few blood-stained rags. She was discovered by a man driving by who was kind enough to help her. She was taken to a doctor well known for treating many of these women who were brutalized in this way. She not only survived to tell her story, but she is an amazingly strong Christian woman who forgave and holds no bitterness against those who brutalized her and murdered everyone she loved.

Many of us were made aware of these types of atrocities on the continent of Africa when the KONY 2012 campaign (the manhunt for Ugandan rebel Joseph Kony) made worldwide headlines. There are stories of other men, women, and children worldwide who are beaten and brutalized. The stories are too numerous to specifically address. Does God care about our earthly suffering? I believe He does wholeheartedly. I believe our lives and deaths have a purpose and sometimes we don't understand.

In a vapor mindset, we may view this kind of earthly suffering as a tragic injustice to our lives and deem it as unfair. We may question in our hearts as to what kind of loving God would allow such suffering and inhumanity. Faith in eternity sees a bigger picture. It doesn't always make the natural, earthly part easier to cope with or understand. I don't believe that our earthly suffering or unanswered prayers in the vapor equate to God's depth of love for us. I also believe God allows our life experiences to equip us with a testimony that "Love conquers all" no matter how horrific we consider our experiences to be.

Romans 8:28 states that all things work together for the good of those who love the Lord, and are called according to His purpose.

Certain situations seem like there could be no good in them whatsoever, but it depends on our perspective.

We all understand earthly pain, some of us more severe than others. However, none of us, including Job in the Bible have been perfect. What about Jesus who was completely sinless? If you've seen the movie, The Passion of the Christ, historians say that the bloody, brutal, beating in the film was likely not as bad as what Jesus may have taken. Whatever the case, Jesus certainly endured His share of earthly suffering without any of His own wrongdoing.

In those times, being arrested was not a pleasant experience to say the least. They did not mirandize a person, cuff them,

THE VAPOR

and escort them in the back of a chariot. It was rough—many were publicly beaten, severely whipped, and dragged to jail. They were put into dark, cramped dungeons with sewage, maggots, and rodents. Prisoners were often chained to walls or to one another with restricted movement. They were often injured and suffered inhumane treatment, starvation, and dehydration.

The conditions they faced make today's prisons seem more like a hotel. Couple that with the fact that Jesus was publicly ridiculed, spat upon, hit with rocks and fists, cursed at, and whipped while being forced to carry a cross that likely weighed 125 pounds for an estimated half a mile. (Now don't get all "factual data funky" with me. These are merely recorded guesses—I don't know and neither do you). Jesus came to simply love, heal, and spread the gospel. He did no earthly wrong, yet He suffered greatly in His 33 years in the vapor. Just as God loved Jesus, He loves us before, during, and after our earthly days.

Neither the depth, nor amount of our earthly suffering reflects God's love, protection, and blessing on us.

Let's face it: We are human, comprised of real flesh and blood. We all have thoughts, emotions, feelings, and conscience. I've always been a pretty compassionate person. I care about people, and I have a loving heart. I think I'm wired a bit differently from many men. I'm as manly as they come now.

WHY ME? LIFE, DEATH, AND STAGES WITHIN THE VAPOR

I'm not metro sexual, or in touch with any feminine side. I'm driven, focused, a bit brash at times, and pretty competitive.

However, my testosterone ends where fairness, compassion, and justice begin. My kids find it humorous that I'll catch a spider in a plastic cup and put it out of the house rather than kill it. Yet on the other hand, they understand if an intruder broke in our home with intent to harm us, I'd give him a dirt nap (end his earthly life) without a second thought before I'd let him harm anyone I love. I enjoy a physical football game that puts great skill and strength on display. I detest the violent, dirty hits (that many men cheer for) resulting in concussions and severe injury.

On a deeper level, when I see pain, suffering, and injustice, it really hits me deeply—I'm moved to compassion. There is very little disconnect, even when I do not know the person(s) involved. They can be half a world away and I can be moved to tears by the pain of other people.

We all experience pain and trauma from the point of conception throughout our lives. They are unavoidable by-products of living on the earth. They are intentional parts of our spiritual development and voyage through the vapor. We adapt, learn to manage, and live with them. We reach a new threshold of understanding when we realize the hard

THE VAPOR

times and trials are merely brief stages, a shorter part of a short vapor.

Furthermore, there is no testimony without a test. Our experiences more often than not, are meant not only for our benefit, but to benefit the paths of others as we all go along on this journey interconnected. God sees, knows, and understands what we go through—better than we can ever comprehend. All of it (no picking or choosing) works to our good and His glory.

CHAPTER 7

Seeing the Vapor for What It Is

We see more fighting, conflict, downright crazy behavior all around us based upon vapor-minded mentality. Perfectly sane people drive themselves into behaving in a manner that would signal mental illness. There are those who are absolutely stuck in vapor vision. We've heard of people killing one another over territory, love, hate, a pair of shoes, greed, jealousy, and race. Racism has been a hot button as long as different races of men have walked the earth. As an African American, please give me just a little latitude to delve a bit into this issue, as it has affected my earthly life and those of many others. Racism is a clever trick of our enemy. He uses the diversity God intended to be beautiful and meaningful, and twists it into ugly lines of division to keep us distracted from our destiny.

Rev. Dr. Martin Luther King, Jr. was really onto something with his "I Have A Dream" speech and philosophy. It seemed many

THE VAPOR

whites, including Christians, simply could not bring themselves to see African Americans as people—just like them. Racism isn't reserved for America, or just blacks and whites. It takes place all over the world. Whether black, white, brown, or otherwise, each one of us is a living, breathing soul inside. The shell we call the human body is simply the temporary residence of a soul God intended to occupy the earth for a time, and then to later be with Him.

Racism is simply another distraction: a ploy by our enemy intended to keep our eyes focused on skin color, background, or origin rather than eternal destiny.

I've attempted to be mindful of pointing my finger, stating absolutes, or giving orders in this book. I've done what I can to simply build my case and give each reader room to consider. I will briefly cross that line in this one instance. If you carry around bitterness and anger toward any race, you'd better wake up! You may have a perception of someone, but you do not know their story. People are, to a large extent, a product of their upbringing, surroundings, and influences.

You will find sin in every race. You will find vapor-minded and eternal-minded people in every race. You will find realized and unrealized potential in every race. Do recognize that each person you see regardless of their physical appearance is a child of God. Wisely choose your friends and associates. Love everyone, and choose the love of your life according to the way in which God would lead you. If you are in an interracial relationship, feel no condemnation from the folly of vapor-minded scoffers. Do you honestly think God is concerned with the skin color of our spouses? If Jesus finds no condemnation in you, ignore those who do. Choose your love, and then love your choice. Racism is hate, which is the opposite of God who is pure Love.

I want to shake up people I see wandering aimlessly, fighting, bickering, stressed out over this vapor, the economy, the state of the world, etc. and tell them there's more than what you see. I look back on some of my life's emotionally unstable moments and recall flying into fits of rage over silly things. I acted in an utterly embarrassing manner over nothing. Well, nothing but fear, anxiety, insignificance, and other vapor-driven emotions that lead many of us into irrational thoughts, words, and acts. Wow, am I glad no cameras were present. Or perhaps seeing myself afterwards would've been a great lesson. Once you grasp it, you'll want to tell those around you, "C'mon people ... it's like the matrix and the blue pill."

We even quibble over vapor within the vapor. We hold grudges over all sorts of things we perceive as big and little. And someone says to us, "In the greater scope of life, does that really matter?" That question can broaden our vision with respect to a relatively minor situation. Perhaps we should

THE VAPOR

consider another question: *Does it really matter to your eternity?* Distractions, distractions—another way our enemy keeps our eyes away from the eternal prize.

When we understand the vapor for what it is, it helps us in true forgiveness and letting go of hurts. Those of us that have been hurt or crossed by others in some way tend to forgive with our lips. Oh, we say we forgive those that wronged us, but our hearts sometimes tell another story. Have we truly let go of those hurts? When the name of the offender(s) is mentioned, does our neck hair stand up? I can honestly say that I've been hurt many times in my life. I view those hurts from a different perspective. Just as the vapor, hurts and offenses are quick passing moments.

In our vapor mentality, it can seem like a broken heart will never heal. Bitterness and anger are so easy to hold on to. Spite and even revenge can actually seem rewarding in a vapor mindset. There are many fantastic reads on forgiveness available, and I'd suggest diving in if forgiving others is a struggle for you. Remember to apply an eternal mindset to what you learn.

Seeing the vapor for what it is keeps our focus sharp, resulting in great choices and truly successful earthly lives.

God watches us (with infinitely more understanding) in the way we watch our children. Have you ever seen a child throw

SEEING THE VAPOR FOR WHAT IT IS

a tantrum over an ice cream cone falling on the ground? They may roll on the floor, kick, cry, scream, going insane as if it's the last ice cream on earth. They cry passionately. The most important thing in their world, at that time, is the ice cream.

As a parent, we sit and observe, understanding the tantrum is a complete overreaction. We see the ice cream as a little deal, and from our perspective, it seems quite silly that the child is acting in this manner. We (hopefully) stay calm, and in adult-like manner we explain to the child that it's really going to be OK. If they continue acting in this manner, it *will* be the last ice cream on earth. But if they just relax and trust us, perhaps they can have another cone now, later, next time, or whatever. *We see the dropping of an ice cream cone for what it is.* But from the perspective of the child's mind, we adults just don't get it. "No, it won't be OK. No, it wasn't just an ice cream cone. And no, I won't calm down! This is an all-out emergency and the world will know my fury!"

Isn't it ironic that we, as mature adults, can carry ourselves in this childlike fashion? We complain about the things that happen to us and throw our adult tantrums in all sorts of forms. We even withdraw our faith from a God that understands and loves us more than we could ever love our own children or comprehend. He looks over us and the way we stress out over vapor-related issues. God reminds

THE VAPOR

us that no matter what we face, no matter how much drama we drum up, *"It's only ice cream."*

We have a tendency to make our earthly lives so complex. In the quest to continue improving our vapor, we frequently miss unbelievable experiences right in front of us. We want to achieve a certain status we see others living—what we perceive as the "good life." The "grass is greener" thing paralyzes us. The shame is, we get so caught up in our neighbor's grass, we miss our own.

We see other people and think, "Wow, their lives are so awesome, if I could only be where they are." We see them publicly in their best moments—all dressed up, all smiles, and seemingly without a problem in the world. We tend to compare the highlight reel of others to our own extra footage (another Steven Furtick-ism). We don't see their challenging moments, dark hours, or bad hair days. Perhaps they have found a way to simply manage the issues and enjoy life, regardless of circumstance. Despite the appearance of some of our perfect lives, perfect children, perfect jobs, cars, homes, etc. We all have issues and are more alike than we imagine.

I saw a commercial for the BET (Black Entertainment Television) awards with Actor/Rap Artist Will Smith and his family that really exemplifies this point. Will, his lovely

SEEING THE VAPOR FOR WHAT IT IS

wife Jada, and all of their adorable children were dressed in white, filming a commercial for the awards show. They were all smiles, in perfect poses, announcing the awards show together—a Kodak moment of the "perfect" family. Suddenly, one of the kids told another to move; the other replied, "Shut up!" then Will and Jada jumped in! It pretty much became an all-out brawl, ending with them all storming offstage.

Yes, this was a staged argument, but I'm sure there was some truth to it. It was a cool moment, where they shared with the world the fact that money, fame, and all the accolades don't exempt them from real life and experiences we all have. The fact is, none of us have perfect lives. In our imperfection we find a humanity and vulnerability that make us real—dependent on each other and God. The choices we make based upon our perspectives dramatically impact the outcome of our earthly lives.

Our vapor or eternal perspective determines our perception of the severity of our earthly issues.

Fear is the common denominator in our misperception of the vapor. We lack faith due to fear of being wrong. We fear things we do not comprehend or understand. We fear the unknown. We fear insecurity and insignificance. Let's briefly detour and follow the trail of fear. Let's keep it very relatable to today's everyday American.

THE VAPOR

Jim fears losing his job, why? If Jim loses his job, he'll lose his income. OK, then what? He may not be able to find work again soon. OK, then what? He will get behind on house and car payments. OK, then? His credit goes bad, he may lose the house and car. Then? He is forced to move, live with others, and make changes to his and his family's lifestyle. Then? He and his family could go hungry, need welfare, food banks, or shelter. Then? People will think of him differently, and perhaps see him as a failure. Then?

Hmm ... We're not sure what follows, but understand the point. First, look how far our imagination can take us. Second, examine everything Jim has to lose. Which of these things are tied into his eternity? Finally, which of these things should his joy be based upon? House? Car? Credit? People's opinions? When we put our faith in ourselves, stuff can become "mini-gods" and thus our joy is attached to them. Joy can be independent of things when our faith is in God and our focus is on His eternal plan.

Fear extinguishes joy. Fear is not from God. Joy cannot flow from fear.

The eternal mindset is freedom from judgment and contempt of others. It lifts the burdens of keeping up with the Joneses. It helps us to be less judgmental. It differs from a person that simply doesn't care what people think. The eternally-minded are aware and care deeply about the eternity of others. They want others to understand. Without pressure or judgment, they seek to gently and lovingly shift vapor-minded people into eternal thinking. The eternal mindset seeks to accomplish these setting examples of grace, humility, and love. They understand the importance of the vapor of others, and its impact on eternity. The key is, the eternal mindset keeps the perspective. It reflects in their speech and actions, and that sense of peace is what draws people. It makes us really comfortable in our own skin.

People could see the difference in Jesus and they flocked to Him. Yes, many sought His wisdom. Yes, many sought healing and miracles. There were many who simply sought to believe. It is no different today. *People want to believe. People are thirsty for living water.* How cool would it be for *us to deliver that water?* People should see the modern-day Christian and see peace in the chaotic world around us. If the world sees us as needy, clingy, beggars clinging to God for a better vapor, then they will not be inspired to follow.

The modern day church should be like a lighthouse on a hill. In fact, a lighthouse with a swanky restaurant. When the hungry, thirsty, and weary come, we should be like waiters. We should put zero emphasis on their race, background, financial status, physical appearance, and other vapor stuff. We should welcome them into the lighthouse with a comfy seat, serve them water, followed by the finest meal, and then offer them a place to rest.

Then we should waive the entire bill. It should be completely "on the house." When we get to this selfless place, we begin to model Jesus, and that is the original intent for our earthly lives.

The sooner we make the shift, the more of our earthly lives we can use for the intended purpose.

Our vapor has an intended flow. We are born. We reach the age of decision, understanding, and discover our talents and gifts. We at some point are given the opportunity to choose our spiritual path. We commit our lives to God's path that maximizes our gifts. The fruit of our lives should glorify God—bring our eternity and the eternity of others closer to Him. We have relationship with God and others. We trust Him through the journey during the good, bad, and all in between.

Consult and acknowledge God in all we do. We then pass the message to others that we need to love God. We love and build one another. We help each other to find our gifts and purpose. We collectively recognize and effectively walk out the vapor. We reach the end of the vapor. God tells us, " Job well done" and we spend eternity with Him.

Relatively simple, but not always easy. It takes faith, commitment, and sacrifice. We claim we want success and want to run the race of life well. Those who realize *who they are* and *Whose they are* desire spiritual success as well.

CHAPTER 8

Getting the Vapor Right

Once we know who we truly are, we work on eternity and the vapor just follows. It is squarely on your shoulders to find out these truths and decide whether or not to develop your relationship with God. If you choose, say this out loud with all sincerity: *"Lord Jesus, here I am imperfect, lost, and in need of You. I invite You into my life to be the true Master and Leader of my life. Forgive me for every misstep You define as sin. Please replace everything in my heart with Your truth, Your Love, and let my earthly life follow Your purpose to eternity. In Jesus' name, amen."*

Now throw out your past like last week's trash. *All of it.* What you did a minute ago, yesterday, or yesteryear, (no matter how "bad" you think it was) God forgives you and isn't mad. Oh, and here's a bonus: He won't throw it back in your face like some people do.

When people say God will judge us, I firmly believe it is absolutely true. However, I do not believe we are going on trial for our past sins. I believe this to be a huge misconception. If that were true, I'd say everyone from Mother Teresa on down, will simply fall short. I also do not believe God is going to put our earthly choices on the "sin-o-meter," or "totem pole of big and little sins." I don't believe He will say: "Well ... John over here only thought bad thoughts, but over here Charlie robbed a bank. So, John, you're in. And since you were *really* bad—sorry, Charlie."

I believe God will examine our hearts, weigh it against the knowledge we acquired, and decisions we made based upon that knowledge. Did we intend to love God with all our heart, mind, and soul? Did we intend to love our neighbor as ourselves? Did we intend to keep His word hidden in our hearts so that our lives would be more pleasing to Him? I keep using the word "intend" as none of us can flawlessly accomplish any of the above.

I believe God understands us. I believe He's a righteous and just God who won't wait till we get to the end of our earthly lives and say "Aha, gotcha! You didn't do X, Y, or Z, so off you go." I believe He wants us to succeed in this walk. I'm careful to say "I believe," as I'm not attempting to "put words into God's mouth" or pretend I have some deep revelation no one else has. This is simply my belief, based upon what I've derived from God's word, which I receive as truth.

The onus is on you to seek truth for yourself and develop your own personal relationship with God. From my perspective, it is relatively straightforward. Read your Bible and other books about the Bible to gain knowledge. Live according to His word by faith. Pray for understanding, then accept that you will never understand it all. As simple as it may seem, again I say I have not found it to be easy. I have found that it requires hard work, discipline, and faith for all of which I pray God would renew my mind daily.

God knew we would not have all the answers. He knew we would make mistakes. He only asks that we repent, believe, walk by faith, apply His word, and depend on His grace.

God knows I've thought to myself many times, "God, why don't You just make this thing plain to us? Why don't you just show up in the sky, on TV, or like Morgan Freeman in Bruce Almighty, spend a week with each of us, and tell us what to do? Isn't it a little unfair to give us a life that's full of flaws, with no instruction manual, and then expect us to find our way through it all?" I believe it goes right back to faith. It requires little faith to believe in someone or something you have seen.

Again, just my humble opinion, but I think God knew we'd go through this journey with lots of questions and doubts. I think He knew we'd in some cases, even perhaps doubt His very existence. God knew the courage it would take for us to ask Him to transform our hearts. He knew we'd have to be willing to open up Pandora's Box and deal with the stuff we'd rather bury inside and pretend doesn't exist. He knows all the goofy thoughts going on in our minds. We can't trick Him when our lips utter words and our heart is in an entirely different place. I firmly believe God wants relationship with us based upon faith, love, and our choosing to be in fellowship with Him.

One of the most important and awesome powers God gave us is the power to choose. We can choose to follow or decline, sort of like Twitter. I don't use that analogy to trivialize such a monumental decision, but merely to simplify it. Once we decide to follow someone on Twitter, we begin to see the posts in their feed or stream of tweets. When we decide to follow Jesus, we open ourselves up to God's life feed. We then begin to understand our purpose and how to walk in it. Knowing and making the decision is only half the battle. *The rubber meets the road when we follow* (don't miss that). "Following," to name a few steps, include: joining a local church, serving, inviting the lost, studying the Bible (God's word), and walking with God.

Deciding to follow and following are two vastly different steps. For years, I've been working on my friend Drew to get him to commit his life to God. He came to church with me a couple times over the years. He heard good stuff, thought it all made sense, but he hadn't yet taken the next step of deciding to follow. He started coming a little more regularly, and then one day he heard a message that really applied to his current life situation. He then decided to follow, and I was so pumped! He even gave his information after church to the support team. And I thought, "Yep, he's in there!" Then he stopped coming, as in—that was his last visit. I continued to invite him but didn't press, I sort of backed off. It seemed something in him was reluctant to go from "deciding to follow" to the *"action of following."*

The point behind this story is the choice. My friend is equipped with enough information to make a decision to follow, but he hasn't committed to the act of following. He had a choice when I brought him to church. He had a choice when he chose to follow, and whether or not to continue following. Provided he is granted the next few months of life, he will have another opportunity to choose once I hand him a copy of this book. We each have choices as well: the choice to believe or not believe, as well as the structure of our vapor and eternity.

Following Jesus is a conscious decision, an additional step that comes after the decision to follow. It is imperative to teach our children how to decide, then act on their decisions.

THE VAPOR

Think of how we raise our children. The vapor mentality is ingrained in us by our parents and society. We live it, have kids, rinse, and repeat. We have to be mindful in what and how we teach our children. We have to show them with our lives and actions, that real commitment goes beyond lip service. They should see our example and understand the importance of excellence. They should understand service of others, grace, and gratitude. They should love life and not fear death. They should know life is but a vapor, preparing them for eternity.

We do our children a huge disservice by giving them everything when they are young. They begin to equate receiving to love. As we reflect on our parents love, we think of all they did for us. Our perception of our parents' love is: "You gave me life, you gave me milk. You gave me love, hugs, and kisses. You gave me band-aids when I fell. You bought me bikes, trains, and video games. You did so much for me."

Notice a pattern? Gimme, gimme, gimme! We had a saying where I grew up, when kids would continually say to adults, "Gimme this" or "Gimme that." They'd reply, "Gimme got shot!" Many of us thought it was just a quip to say "no" to us. I now see it as elders in their wisdom making a point. We always sought to get something. Was our love based upon always receiving? When the faucet was shut off, or when "Gimme got shot," did it change the way we felt or perceived the relationship?

GETTING THE VAPOR RIGHT

Our perception of love develops in a self-centered, vapor-focused manner.

We seldom define love by what we give. God is Pure Love, and God is about giving. He gave His Son to pay the price for our shortcomings. Is it any wonder most of us have such a hard time seeing life for what it truly is, and maximizing it for God and our eternity?

As children, love is defined by what we receive. As adults, love is defined by what we give. The same holds true as we start and mature in our spiritual walk.

We can sometimes look at God like a genie or an ATM, just like our children can sometimes view us. When we spiritually "grow up" just as in the natural, we begin to appreciate what we can give to God. It comes in the form of a strong relationship built on worship, prayer, time, fasting, tithing, and love. So how do we get the vapor right? I certainly don't claim to have the exact answer. And for that matter, I don't know that there is one simple answer. The answer could have as many variables as there are people on the planet.

Here is a question I pose: Is the purpose of our vapor to grow up, go to school, get a job, a spouse, a house, a car, have 2.5 kids, go to church, retire, pass the baton, then pass on? In many of our lives all of the above will happen, but just like a job, skin color, or background, these things do not define us nor do they define our destiny. I suggest that all of it, even our very own lives, are temporary and meant for God's glory.

C'mon, what is a permanent job position? Permanent make-up? Dentures? Portfolios? These terms exemplify the vapor-minded mentality that society has adopted as truth, and many of us have bought into. The dictionary definition of "permanent" is: *existing perpetually, everlasting without significant change.* I submit to you when you quit, get fired, promoted, laid off, or die, or your job position becomes a little less permanent—none of the above-mentioned things are permanent, nor are many of the things we label permanent. That thinking is the essence of what gets us into the mindset of accumulating, stockpiling, building monuments, and believing "It's ours forever!"

Everything on the earth is here for us and we are to take dominion. But we have to keep it straight in our minds—things are only on loan to us. We rule the stuff, but God owns it.

The earth is the Lord's and the fullness thereof. — Psalm 24:1

None of us can hold onto a single material thing beyond our vapor. Sure, we can hand it down the family line but we no longer have control. One day, Warren Buffet and Bill Gates will see the last day of their vapor, and they will no

GETTING THE VAPOR RIGHT

longer control the material possessions or vast wealth they have accumulated. Philanthropists seem to get this concept. When they pass, a certain amount may go to family, but the vast majority goes back into the pool in which it was created (hopefully for the betterment of many), rather than attempting to hoard it all in their families or a small group.

When we shift from the vapor-minded mentality, we lessen the importance on the stockpile, and see a bigger picture.

In the midst of all the distraction and daily life, we cannot miss the fact our lives have God-given purpose. Earthly goals are fantastic. Education; money; physical, mental, and emotional health; family; management of stress and distractions—they all come while navigating our way through the vapor. Yes, yes, YES, these are a part of shaping our destiny. When we keep our perspective, glorify God, and make great choices, all of the education, money, and other attributes can help smooth out uncertain terrain in our journey. That said, they are not a substitute for eternal thinking.

It can be challenging to shift from a vapor mindset. Despite our vapor-minded perspective that the ones with the most money have it "easy"—it is not always so. Wealth can hinder us, and provide us an "alternative" to trusting or depending on God. Money, education, and position can become our source and cause us to rely on ourselves solely. They can also cause us to be spiritually stagnant and lazy. Lack, unchecked desire, and pursuit of finances can present the same challenges. The key is maintaining joy and an eternal perspective on life's variables and purpose.

Money can make our vapor more pleasure-filled. The insatiable quest for more pleasure can cause us to drift far away from God's purpose.

We literally owe it to God to use our vapor wisely and productively. Clearly those with an eternal mindset understand the call to excellence. We should answer that call based upon our gifts. We don't have the luxury to spend life wasting our gifts in a manner that dismisses the Giver. We shouldn't feel like it's "our life" to do "whatever we wanna."

God has given us choice and we are able to go about life as we please. We can even choose to end our own lives. I firmly believe suicide is an insult to the great investment God made in us, and the awesome gift of life God gave to us. In some cases, it is a by-product of confusion, or of a lack of purpose. In all cases, it is a derivative of insecurity and insignificance.

Purpose gives us reason to keep living, fighting, walking out our vapor filled with faith. In most cases, I view suicide as a lazy, cowardly way out of the work, faith, and commitment

GETTING THE VAPOR RIGHT

required to live. That sounds a bit harsh, but truth can be harsh. All sin grieves God's heart, but suicide literally impacts destiny. Suicide, murder, and abortion alter the destiny of those involved and the lives of those whose paths they may have affected.

Life is a gift, and God made a tremendous investment in us. We don't have the luxury to waste the gift.

Getting the vapor right takes prayer, faith, and love. This is absolutely true. However, we cannot discount the fact it also takes good old-fashioned hard work, commitment, and pursuit of greatness. Not all of us start out in the same position, situation, and with equal opportunity. Some of us start the race tripped-out of the starting blocks or far behind. Some of our challenges are greater than others.

The good news is that nothing is new under the sun, and we can all learn from one another's experiences. We have to kick in our will, heart, desire, and faith. For a great earthly life, we have to avoid laziness and complacency. I frequently tell my children (they'll smile or possibly cringe when they read this): *We cannot put forth an average effort and expect an exceptional result.* The reality is, greatness in our vapor and our eternity are not simply handed to us—they take work.

THE VAPOR

When asked the question, "Do you want success?", almost everyone would say, "Yes." Before this reading, I'd imagine most would assume I mean vapor success, but here's my point: *Spiritual, eternal, or vapor success each take the aforementioned hard work and commitment.* Truthfully, many of us love pleasure more than success. We talk a great game, but as the old saying goes, "Talk is cheap." The biggest contributing factor in our failure and unhappiness is allowing what we want *now*, to take precedent over what we want *most*.

CHAPTER 9

Yes, Enjoy the Vapor

Ahh, here's the part we all are waiting for. Here is your chapter. Now we dive into the good stuff: fun, pleasure, and enjoyment! I hope at no time in this book I insinuated that earthly life was not intended to have pleasure. Every day that God grants us—in fact, every breath is a gift, not a guarantee. Pleasure and enjoyment are a part of our vapor. We are to enjoy beauty, relationships, and all good things here in the world. God created us with pleasure receptors in our bodies. He completely understood what we'd like, dislike, struggle with, etc. When we know Him, we understand He's not a strict, harsh dictator who loves only "good" people and sends everyone else to hell. I don't believe He in fact "sends" people to hell, I believe He allows us to choose our destiny. God knew we wouldn't be perfect. I don't imagine Him sitting with His hand on the cover of His big red zapper waiting for us to err in our ways.

THE VAPOR

Within the context of reaching our purpose for our earthly lives, God intended for us to enjoy our vapor. All of the beauty of this planet is ours. From the beginning, God gave us dominion and power to rule and enjoy His promises in our earthly lives.

Genesis 1:28 says that we are to be fruitful, multiply (increase in number), subdue the earth, rule over the fish in the sea, the birds in the air, and over every creature that moves on the ground.

That's right, everything on the earth is here for us to enjoy, and take dominion. All of the natural beauty that we find pleasing to our eyes is created to add to our vapor experience. Everything God gifted man to create is here for us to enjoy. Beautiful buildings, architecture, Range Rovers, mansions, resorts, relationships, love, whatever we desire—enjoy, appreciate, share. Yes, align it with God's will and let it be a part of our vapor.

Wait a minute, hold on … Does this make money the dominant factor of a great earthly life? Hardly not! Let's put it in park again. It is OK to set goals and have stuff, just keep in mind the "why." Understand that even with all the planning, we cannot make our plan outside of God's plan. We are not on our own time, folks. (We'll address that more in a bit.) What is your motive for what you do? Examine your heart, and frequently reexamine it.

YES, ENJOY THE VAPOR

Possessions, relaxation, and enjoyment should refresh and invigorate us. Pleasure and rest should serve as a plateau, then a springboard to the next level of our journey.

Are we seeking happiness? No one is always happy. "Happy" is a fleeting thing. My daughter will be happy when I buy her a puppy (yes, honey, Dad will buy you a puppy). But she may not be happy when it's naughty or has an accident. She will, however, experience joy in her relationship with the puppy—completely unrelated to the happiness.

Will possessions keep us happy when we lose loved ones, become ill, or battle tough times? What we truly seek is peace and joy. So many of us think that money will give us the peace and joy we desire. The underlying issue is, money will not solve our insignificance issues or vapor-lack mentality. We picture ourselves on a beach in Waikiki, fanning our faces with hundred dollar bills, holding our drinks topped with tiny umbrellas. Is this the example Jesus set for us? We don't see the load of stress that accompanies managing and maintaining wealth.

TD Jakes put it so well in saying, "You see me up here in this suit, you hear all the applause, see the accolades, and you think you want this, but you don't want this." People don't see his 18-hour days, the weight of so many people's issues, the criticism, or the heavy load of responsibilities. He went on to say

THE VAPOR

"If I were to ever throw you the keys (to my life), I'd advise you to duck. Just let 'em fly by, because you don't want this."

Prosperity comes at a price. Consider carefully the risks and rewards of vapor wealth.

Take a look at some of the lives of those who seemingly "have it all." On the surface, it looks so tasty, pleasure-filled, and great. Is it leading them to or away from their eternity in God? Are their lives peaceful, joyful, and vibrant? Are the parties, possessions, and posturing simply an attempt to fill a spiritual void with temporary things? It is not to say that none of the financially well-off folks have joy and peace, that is obviously not true. It's awesome when one can achieve peace and joy and have the financial abundance. How much more awesome when we can have joy and peace regardless of the size of our stockpiles?

Money is important. However, it is not the key to peace and joy. Real joy and peace are found in connection to our Creator and His purpose. Peace and joy are independent of financial status.

Peace comes when we are aligned with our purpose and Creator. Joy comes from relationship with God and one another. God is Love. Jesus is Love, real Agape Love in its purest form. That's the missing "thing" people are searching for. Rich, poor, and in between, we all seek to fill that void.

YES, ENJOY THE VAPOR

It keeps us exploring, experimenting, and hunting. The danger in financial abundance is we can attempt to fill the void (and even believe it's filled) by the fleeting things money can buy. Without a doubt, this creates a further disconnect from God as we rely on our stuff as our source.

We are thrive-connected to God like a branch thrives connected to a tree. Our lives should be of constant growth, development, and change. Our lives should have peace and joy. We should enjoy where we are, simultaneously focused on where we aim to go. There is pain, pleasure, excitement, disappointment, and other emotions in every stage of our vapor. If we are not careful, we can spend our lives in a constant pursuit of "happy days and better vapor," never enjoying where we are. Our joy and peace should not be tied to our position. We must challenge ourselves. Our goals for God ought to be so lofty, only an act of God will bring them to fruition. Then, we are not only using our potential, but putting ourselves in position to rely on God.

During the ride however, we should not forget to stop. And as they say, "Smell the roses."

Have you ever walked a path you normally drive everyday? Notice how many new things you see, hear, and smell that you miss when you're in the car? You notice flowers, plants, fences, the neighbor with the red door, and the size of the

THE VAPOR

tree that started so small, years ago. You notice cracks in the sidewalk, ivy growing up the lattice on another house, the lady working in her garden, or the one sitting on her porch sipping lemonade. All were there yesterday, but you whizzed by it all in your haste to get wherever you were going.

The same holds true in the rat race of our earthly lives. We get going into a routine and all the details become a blur. Life begins to be predictable and (yawn) boring. Moreover, we get desensitized to all of the simple but incredible beauty around us. We no longer appreciate the simple joys; we're constantly seeking the "new thing." It causes us to take people, situations, even life itself for granted. What a waste, what a shame, what disrespect to such a precious and significant phase!

This planet has so many beautiful places, people, and things—all of which God created for His glory and our pleasure. If the Earth isn't enough to tickle your fancy, we're on the cusp of public space travel. It is ours to enjoy. God intended us in all of our diverse tastes to enjoy His wonders. Why miss out? None of us can take it all in, but certainly we can get more out of what we do experience.

If it is not in God's will, I may never visit all of the beautiful places Deepak Chopra has seen in his lifetime. However, I can certainly choose to spend my time connected to God which helps deepen my perception of the beauty in my life everyday. I will certainly strive to see more places to enjoy and be in awe of what my God has done. I will give Him glory for what He has created. I will appreciate with joy, the beauty of the days and places God allows me to see and experience.

Yes, this life is but a short vapor, but the vapor is significant and meant to be enjoyed. We all get a life, but do we all truly live?

Rather than a "bucket list," why wait? Make a "life list" of places to go, experiences to have, people with whom to experience these things with (kept in the context of God's will and purpose). Make sure to include your dream locations and activities on that list. Hang glide in Maui, skydive in Toledo, go up in a hot air balloon over the coast of Italy, sail the world, swim with dolphins off the Miami coast. *Dream it, plan it, God willing—do it! Just don't obsess over it or miss the simple joys we are surrounded by on a day-to-day basis in the interim.*

With proper balance, planning, and enough days granted by God, we should make a sizable dent in that list. Life is not a long pleasure party when we are in God's will. Life is a journey full of ups, downs, twists and turns. We are not going to be happy or comfortable in every moment. We will have to work, walk on faith, endure doubt, and so much more. No matter the number of our days, we should have appreciation, peace, and joy throughout the journey.

THE VAPOR

Some of life's greatest moments of joy are found in the most simple of things. I sometimes step outside on my porch to enjoy a simple deep breath and stretch with the sunshine on my face. I put a simple patio set on our deck so my kids and I can enjoy meals outside. Love, giving, and simple moments can bring us some of the greatest pleasure. There's no feeling like a mom's nurturing embrace; a father's comforting voice; or the time we spend together with family and friends laughing, walking, and talking.

There is nothing like the hugs I get from my 6-year-old son. They are amazing. When those little arms wrap around me, and I see that smile of his, it brings so much joy to my heart. When my kids and I get cozy on the couch with a bowl of popcorn and a movie, or play a board game, we take simple moments and create joy-filled lasting memories. I enjoy the beauty of the Pacific Northwest where I live with its trees, snow-capped mountains, rivers, lakes, forests, flowers, and hills.

Most of the simple things cost us very little other than the time to slow down and enjoy them. We may at some point enjoy Waikiki or even Dubai as a family, but I'm not obsessed with it. I refuse to miss out on the beauty and greatness all around me in pursuit of what I see others doing. These are simply short moments within a short vapor. I am choosing not to miss out on a moment of my joy coveting someone else's vapor. Most of all, I choose not to miss out on my calling for my life in pursuit of fleeting things that are not eternal.

Life already has enough complexity. Find joy in the simple things.

Young people, start young. If you are no longer in your 20's, cool ... start right where you are. Study, read, pray, and discover God's purpose for your life. Plan your life according to God's plan for you, and you will have found your flow. The sooner you find your flow, the more of your life on earth you get to spend in it. The longer you are in your flow, the more your potential and accomplishments multiply.

The amazing thing is when you are in God's plan, joy and peace naturally come along. It is said that when you find a career in what you love and are passionate about, then you'll never again work a day in your life. Obviously this isn't meant literally, but when you enjoy what you do every day, it can increase your peace and decrease anxiety exponentially. Your vapor should be an exciting, challenging, amazing experience.

God's career path for us is typically something we enjoy, are proficient at, and what others observe we do well. When it's God's plan, it will likely provide the financial means to meet the desires of your heart. Or God will provide you with entrepreneurial ideas to augment what you do. If it doesn't work out as we expected, His grace is sufficient and we should still have our joy.

THE VAPOR

Enjoy success, learn from it as well as from failure. Consider how much you take on, how much you press, and most of all be acutely aware of the motivating factors behind what you do. Embrace your present and look in hopeful anticipation to your future. In all cases, serve your employers, employees, customers, clients, everyone else around you with a good spirit and heart. Give, receive, love, and serve with grace-filled humility and excellence. Live a great earthly life.

Joy and good countenance tend to bring out the best in us. Smile. Enjoy each day, each hour, and each breath. Learn to look at the great things in your life. With enough effort, you can find plenty of bad and good in just about any situation, whether sold out to either a vapor-mindset or eternal-mindset. We've got one "go round" in the vapor. Treat it as such and make the existence exciting, enjoyable, and productive.

I realize I have to take time for myself. I understand "aggressive," "roll up the sleeves," "run hard," "elbow-grease" phases are essential. No less essential are the "ahh" moments, sitting in the shade, sipping lemonade. What's really awesome is I feel God will place the right balance in my heart.
God's presence is the ultimate great joy of life. For myself, relationship with God fills the void and allows joy to replace "happy." I can almost physically feel when I'm on course with God's plan or when I'm a little (or a lot) off course. You know how you just sort of "know"? It's sort of like when

I pick up a pen, I don't have to think which hand it's in. I'm right-handed, so I just know when the pen is in my right hand, it has a "rightness" to it. That's the best way I can explain how God speaks to my heart. I don't hear an audible voice. I guess I feel a "tug" in my heart, I sort of just know. When we allow our good, bad, strong, weak, talents, and shortcomings to roll into God's plan for us, we can truly enjoy the precursor to eternity.

THE VAPOR

CHAPTER 10

The Vapor is Important, Significant, and Has a Purpose

OK—here's the "ta-da," the fireworks, the grand finale, the pinnacle of the vapor you absolutely MUST grasp. You ready? OK, here it is:

The vapor is extremely important, the decisions you make here will determine the rest of your eternity. Our purpose is to follow Jesus and lead others to do the same. The rest is just details.

We get the choice to select or reject God and His plan. Although this life is a vapor, it is of utmost importance and significance. We must reconcile ourselves and others to our Creator. We must seek God's purpose for our lives then use the gifts and talents He gave us to achieve that purpose. As I mentioned early on, you have fully ingested the red pill at this point. You now have full responsibility of the knowledge—no going back now.

THE VAPOR

God authored a plan for our lives. We, as well, author a plan for our lives. Our troubles reside in the gap between the two.

Don't miss the depth and richness of our life experience on earth. The key is maintaining balance, and keeping our eternal mindset. We should consider the energy we deposit into the vapor and the issues surrounding it. We have to be careful not to let wealth, status, and earthly possessions become mini-gods to us. When we understand perspective and purpose, we have it made in the shade.

Remember, *you rule your choices in the vapor, and Jesus rules you.* Perfect chain of command. Our enemy uses the world system, mindset, and vapor "stuff" in subtle and sometimes very blatant ways. He has one goal in mind—to guide us as far away from God's plan as possible.

We have to remind ourselves God is in control. He gave us rule over the earth and its system. God made us in His likeness. We are in the world but not conformed to the world.

God made a tremendous investment in our earthy lives. Like any good investor, He expects profitable return. In the Bible (Matthew 25:14–30), Jesus tells the parable (story) of the talents. Three men were left with various amounts of money by their master and expected to produce a return. Read it for yourself if you haven't already, and read it again

THE VAPOR IS IMPORTANT, SIGNIFICANT, AND HAS A PURPOSE

if you have. It exemplifies the purpose of the earthly gifts and talents we have. We are not to bury them or keep them to ourselves, rather to take them out in the world, and multiply them to the glory of our Creator. This further substantiates we certainly should not dismiss the importance of the vapor or deem it as insignificant.

It is not time to go "Lion King, hakuna matata," whatever will be, no worries, etc. God gave us all skill sets and gifts that are as unique as our fingerprint. We have been issued a vastly complex temporary life unit which we call the human body. Our bodies, minds, skills, and gifts represent God's huge investment in us. Understand, there is a treasure inside of you, and it means more to yourself and others than you may know. Your life has high value, great destiny, and phenomenal purpose.

The purpose of your life will likely serve the needs of many others you don't even know, in ways you never knew possible.

What is the difference among the world-changing people who seem to maximize their potential? In most cases, they have two arms, two legs, a brain, and 24 hours in a day like most people. But for some reason, they are able to somehow break through and shift to a gear that takes them to the top. Sure, some of it depends on circumstances, where God would have us born, to whom, etc. Let's face it, if Bill Gates were born in a remote village in South America, his life would likely be radically different. However, great people somehow seem to find the cracks in the matrix, the smallest of windows of opportunity, and they turn them into something completely unprecedented. Think of some of the fascinating stories we've heard of people from all over the world who start out in dire conditions, lack education or resources, yet they simply find a way. They tap into their God-given gift and they *maximize it.*

People wonder why certain individuals get the fame and the fortune even when they don't believe in God or follow Jesus. There are also people who get fame and fortune who do believe and follow. It leads me to believe that God is less concerned about the sizzle or sparkle of the vapor, and more concerned about His relationship with us.

God is pure Love and a giver. I don't gather He necessarily takes away our gifts because we don't follow Him. Those who work in their God-given gifts, regardless of their choice to believe in God, serve Him, etc. will enjoy the fruits of their labor. God is not impulsive, and I'm sure He knew exactly what He was doing when He gave each of us our talents and gifts. We may miss it, but God certainly understands that we're dealing with Monopoly money. When the game is over, *all pieces* go back in the box.

God gives each of us the power to choose our path and destiny. Perhaps that's why we are instructed not to worry about

THE VAPOR IS IMPORTANT, SIGNIFICANT, AND HAS A PURPOSE

the wicked or greedy. Some people get the idea, but haven't made the shift away from primarily vapor-focused thinking. I can't say this enough: Maximize the vapor; use God's gift(s) early and often. And God willing, turn a profit with this life. Just don't lose perspective of what the vapor truly is in the process. We should take the time for true relationship with God, serve Him in such a way that He will tell us, "Job well done, humble and faithful servant," when our earthly lives are over.

The vapor is the vehicle to our eternity, the rearview mirror is the past, and the windshield is the future. We should spend less time in the rearview mirror, more in the windshield in order to reach our destiny.

This book started as an inkling, one thought, which quickly became an avalanche. It started with two men sitting in a Starbucks in Seattle, talking over life. The conversation wasn't even intended to go where it went. John and I intended on connecting to get to know one another. I had the idea of finding the right people or combination of people to help me get my struggling music career back off the ground. I experienced a little wave, and I was anticipating catching that one more wave, that last "go round" that would get me where I wanted to be.

I wanted to taste that "good life" one more time. I have great material—everyone thinks the world of me as a performer and

THE VAPOR

writer. All I needed was one more "go round" and this time, I was going to get it right. Here I was, randomly turning over rocks, hoping to find the Staples "Easy" button to get a bit more sizzle out of my vapor. Then, just a little inkling, a comment John made turned it all upside down and inspired this book.

I remember how it felt the days after John and I met, and how the inkling placed a seed in my spirit. I vividly recall the overwhelming feeling as the seed began to grow. It was like I had been seeing life through a pair of dark sunglasses, and then suddenly removed them. I was literally thinking to myself, "Wow, how could I have not understood this before?" It had been right in front of my face the entire time.

Once the concept hit me, it was like a ton of bricks—it immediately rocked my whole thought process. It began to affect the way I spoke, listened, and reacted to everything, even the way I parented. I started processing everything with somewhat of an internal "vapor/eternity separator." I saw life in a totally different light. When issues came my way, I could quickly classify them as vapor or eternal, and my reactions began to reflect eternal thinking. I found a new sense of peace in most of what used to upset me.

When I felt the call to write this book, I remember the exact moment vividly. I was driving, thinking over my life, along with newfound purpose and perspective. I thought over how

THE VAPOR IS IMPORTANT, SIGNIFICANT, AND HAS A PURPOSE

badly I'd missed the mark in my life, relationships, and how my missing the mark affected others around me. Tears began to flow down my face, partially from sorrow. I knew I had to go back and fix a lot of internal and external damage that was a direct result of my vapor mentality. I also shed tears of joy, understanding that I got to start a new day.

A new chapter had begun in my life, with a new and healthier mentality. I wanted to share with everyone, but it was all so new and my emotions were still very raw. I spoke to a couple of people about my thoughts, and I hope they have forgiven me for what were probably some great thoughts surrounded by a bunch of gibberish. I knew I had to organize it all into clear, concise thoughts. An inkling (or seed from God) placed in my heart said a book could reach many people. So I began to write.

We should never discount the inklings in our thought process. They are frequently the voice of God, and we sometimes ignore them because we are lazy, complacent, or fearful. I have had ideas that have been birthed through someone else because of my own lack of taking action. How much further could we have invested in our eternity and the eternity of others? Was our inaction a result of fear of failure? Rejection? The unknown? Success?

Remember the spirit of insecurity and insignificance are the roots of sin. We naturally want to chase the security in

THE VAPOR

what we perceive as "good things" in our vapor mentality. Henry David Thoreau said, "Men spend an entire lifetime fishing, never realizing it was not the fish they were after." We want to be valued and feel secure, but sometimes for the wrong reasons. In a vapor mindset, we place our hope in every fleeting thing rather than trusting in God. Once we truly understand our earthly and eternal purpose, we can grasp the significance of this short window of time, and live it according to God's intended plan. God has a plan and purpose for your life and my life.

CHAPTER 11

God Willing

There are two words we frequently omit when we speak about our lives, our plans, and our futures. Two simple words: *God willing*. This is extremely important. In fact, it should be the common thread of our thoughts, words, actions, and plans for our lives. We love to talk about vision and purpose. We sound so spiritual when we talk about vision and how we plan to accomplish this and that, especially when we tell everyone how much money we plan to make.

Many of us have written down goals, we've been taught by all of the motivational speakers that this is the way to success. We have the plans elaborately laid out. We know exactly how our next two, five, and twenty years will play out. We have simple, prudent strategy so we can set ourselves up for the life we want. We plan to go to school and become doctors, lawyers, athletes, entertainers, climb the corporate ladder, grow a business, etc.

THE VAPOR

We plan to someday have families and live the American dream. We then plan to have enough money to be comfortable in our later vapor years.

All of the retirement commercials tell us to prepare for the future years down the road, and stock up lots of money in investments. God forbid we get sick, or be short on money, and become a burden on our family or society. Nope, surely that is not going to happen to us! Nowhere in our goals do we find the words "God willing" or a Plan B if our lives take an unexpected turn. According to our plans, our younger lives should be mapped out exactly as we decide. And our latter years will look more like a fantasy commercial. We see ourselves riding our red convertible classic car, our spouse under our arm and driving off to the ocean coast—smiling carefree about the happy vapor we have remaining.

With every breath God allows, we are instructed to finish the race strong. And I don't think that meant to hit the gas pedal harder in the convertible. The goal isn't to get wealth, retire, and then quit the race to coast into the sunset. If we attain financial wealth upon retirement, we shouldn't be thinking of how relaxing the rest of our vapor should be.

Money allows us to be a spirit-led part of the solution to problems we see in our families, communities, churches, and world. It can help us to take decisive, real action rather than being stuck in the place of good intentions. Retirement doesn't mean the good fight is over. There are still lost people God wants us to reach. Rather than looking ahead to the remainder of our days as a vacation, we should be thinking "Wow! Now I have money and time to go out and lead the lost to Christ! God willing, I can train up, teach, and support the younger generation to do the same." We should diligently seek the will of God in our lives till our last day.

I have fought the good fight, completed the race, and kept the faith. — 2 Timothy 4:7

Relaxation moments, vacations, traveling and such are fine. However, these should be intervals that refresh us for the next leg of the race. Research it for yourself—people who retire and become completely inactive have far higher numbers of health problems, depression, anxiety, and even die younger. We can only sit around living unfulfilled lives for so long before our minds and bodies begin to erode.

You hear of it all the time where someone retires and they go back to working part-time, simply because they were "bored out of their minds." Perhaps they take up new hobbies, go on new adventures, join a club, or new activities. Our minds need stimulation in order to grow. As we all know, anything that isn't growing is dying. God can use us. Regardless of our circumstances, race, age, or financial status, if we allow it, God can use us till our final breath.

There are some really fascinating people out there, perhaps some you know, preparing for situations they believe may happen. For some it may be Armageddon, The New World Order, The Apocalypse, or some other takeover. For some, it is less intense. They may be buying up gold in belief that the financial system may crash and money will have no value. Many of us have our "number" like the commercial with the guys carrying their cardboard figure to retire comfortably.

Planning, preparation, and goals are a part of prudent wisdom. We should carefully consider our motives in all we do. Every aspect of our lives should directly or indirectly be about bringing souls closer to Christ, staying actively engaged in God's plan.

We are instructed not to worry or hoard onto our stuff. Jesus illustrated the foolishness in building bigger barns to house our crops and possessions. Remember the parable from Luke 12:16-34. What did Jesus tell us to do? Seek His kingdom. Do God's will. If you have tons of finances and stuff—cool, praise Him! If you don't— cool, praise Him just the same! He knows our hearts and may add these things to us, but most importantly He knows our purpose.

Making a profit is not my purpose, it should be a by-product of doing the will of God.

GOD WILLING

Let's take a brief moment to build the context around James 4:14 our key scripture. James 4:13-17 states: Listen, you who are saying, "Today or tomorrow we will go to this city or that city, spend a year there, do business and profit." You do not know what tomorrow will be. For what is your life? It is but a vapor that appears for a little time, then vanishes away. Instead, you should say, "If the Lord wills, we shall live and do this or do that." You boast in your own arrogant plans and ideas. This type of boasting is evil. If anyone knows the good they are to do and does not do it, it is sin. *Ouch.*

We are not in control of our time. Our perception of the future is wrong. We can plan all we'd like to. We must include those two key words in any plan, *"God willing."* Who exactly do we think we are to speak in our own authority with such certainty, telling ourselves and others of our plans to go back to school, spend five years in this position or city?

How can we so confidently make such lofty statements? This is the world's view. People who miss this concept go about the planning of their lives completely disregarding the fact that they don't get to number their own days. Tomorrow is uncertain. We can carefully construct the greatest plans in history, then an accident or illness can change it all. We get such satisfaction out of boasting in our own power. The Bible tells us that all such boasting is evil.

THE VAPOR

Let's take the example of Bill Gates and Steve Jobs. I would venture to guarantee with 100% certainty that both of these intelligent businessmen had big plans. I'm sure we all agree they could not have achieved the level of success in the businesses they founded by simply "winging it." I would venture even further to say with the same certainty that both of these men had plans for their lives that went well beyond 2011. At the time of this writing (2012), Bill Gates is still living. Steve Jobs is not. None of the money, fame, fortune, or possessions that Mr. Jobs' amassed could guarantee that he would see the number of earthly days to fully accomplish his plan.

Our plans can never be guaranteed. God's plan will trump our plan.

We should carefully consider the warnings in the Bible about such blind and sinful boasting. It can be bad news to yourself and others. We have to be wary of teaching and living "a la carte" Christianity, only selecting to live by the parts that benefit the vapor. Woe to us who justify our vapor-minded thinking by removing a scripture from its concept and adding manufactured doctrine.

We'd better let go of the arrogance. We have a "God I got this, but I'll reach out to You when I hit a snag, cause I have a plan" mentality. Plans are fine, but don't forget those two words. Write 'em on your forehead if you have to—*God willing.* Serve God, enjoy your vapor, work, play, do life. Let everything else be a by-product of being in God's will. We are instructed not to chase, covet, be anxious, or compromise for the pleasures of this world. We are not to create our plan and expect God to bring it to pass. We are to seek God, and pray His will be done through us. The rest will be added unto.

God willing I will live here, go there, do this or that. Throughout the books of Romans, Corinthians, and Philippians, as Paul speaks on his intentions or plans, he follows it with "Lord willing", "If it be in God's will" or other forms of the same statement. Here are some scriptures, see for yourself: Romans 1:10, 1 Corinthians 4:19, 1 Corinthians 16:7, Philippians 2:19, 24 and Hebrews 6:3. I love God's word. I love to back up what I say with His word.

We cannot circumvent or manipulate God's will. We set ourselves up for disaster if we ignore it.

If an unexpected circumstance comes such as a job loss, a death, or disease that alters your plan, how will you react? Jesus was willing to endure unimaginable earthly pain and even death for the cause of His Father. What are you willing to do to be in the will of God? What are you willing to surrender?

Our lips say, "God is first, the priority. We trust in Him. Let His will be done in our lives." When we endure difficulty, we

THE VAPOR

have to lean upon the same principle as when we enter the good times. Be committed to God's plan. Rain falls on the just and the unjust. It can ruin one couple's wedding while giving life to the neighboring farmer's crops.

My brethren, count it as joy when you face various trials, in knowledge that the testing of your faith produces patience.
— James 1:2-3

A friend of mine shared with me about his trip to Africa where the children in villages had joy. They had little or no knowledge of all the stuff we covet, but they smiled and praised God. They had simple lives and found simple joys in simple things.

Consider these important questions: Are you OK with God's will? Can you have joy in His plan regardless of circumstances? When you pencil out the plan for your life, are you ready for the heading of your paper to read: *"God willing"* OR will each of your goals begin with *"God willing"?*

CHAPTER 12

The Battle Goes On (yes, for me too)

There is a war in our spirits between vapor-minded thinking and eternal thinking. It is one of the subtle battles our spiritual enemy is fighting against us. Hey, we live in the vapor. We awaken each day to the rigors and trials of our earthly lives. We share the world with people who are not Christian and they are supposed to be vapor-minded. However, we also share the world with and follow Christians who are vapor-minded.

Many of us have spent 20, 30, 40 or more years living in a vapor-minded mentality, and it is very difficult to even begin thinking in an eternal mindset. I find myself talking to Christians about this concept. They understand where I'm coming from, they have their "Aha!" moment. As the conversation continues, you hear all of the pre-programmed vapor mentality still coming from them. It's a tough challenge especially for "seasoned" Christians.

It is similar to that great sermon we hear. We get excited and we say "Amen." We realize its truth and how to apply it to our lives. We leave the church, only to go right back to our same state as before we heard the message. We spend so many years having the vapor mentality drilled into us, that even when we expose it and make the mental shift, we struggle with maintaining an eternal mindset.

Repetition is crucial. An eternal mindset doesn't come overnight for most. Like working out our muscles, it takes consistent effort of training our minds to see life and eternity by faith, for what they are.

Many Christians have been taught sound doctrine from the Bible. The issue resides in the mentality from which much of it is communicated. This is where I perceive an ongoing challenge in the perspective of many well-meaning teachers and the way in which they lead their following believers. Perhaps we need to examine the way in which we communicate the good news, life on earth, and its purpose. Perhaps a shift in thinking can help us more effectively reach the lost. Perhaps it can help shed light on the reasons and rationales behind some of the injustices, the inequalities in the world.

None of us were present to hear Jesus' teachings, but many are recorded in the Bible. I'm not so certain that we didn't miss or misconstrue the fact that Jesus cared first about our eternity.

THE BATTLE GOES ON (YES, FOR ME TOO)

He seemed to have actually taught a lot of the opposite of what we seem to strive for today: the store up, stockpile, maximum-pleasure vapor. He told us how the birds in the air didn't worry for tomorrow and that today has enough troubles. Tomorrow isn't promised.

I gather from what we read in the Bible, we should certainly utilize this earthly life and maximize its potential for its God-defined purpose. That process should not cause us to make earthly life our sole focus. Life should in fact intertwine with the shaping of our eternity.

The Bible is not a vapor-driven book, nor is God vapor-driven. Let's consider the purpose behind this book so many of us have chosen to rely on as God's infallible word. The Bible provides us God's sound advice. It is our guide, it equips us to victoriously maximize God's plan for our eternity. God speaks to us through His Word in the Bible. His Word speaks to our fear, doubt, and issues. It equips and builds us for life.

I have not experienced God in an audible voice. My experience has been more or less a peace in my heart, or an "Aha!" moment. Many times when I read my Bible or pray, I come away with no answers, or more questions than when I started. I'm just being honest. Sometimes I don't know any more than to simply leave my issues or questions with God. Some will tell you the Bible is written and translated by men, so it can't be

ᴛʜᴇ VAPOR

perfect. I say the minds of the authors were no surprise or mystery to God. He already knew exactly what would be written, so don't concern ourselves with the men who wrote or translated.

Pray for wisdom and have faith. Some will tell you the Bible is full of flawed, scientifically impossible stories. Science cannot explain much of what we see today either. I say faith begins where understanding ends. Others will tell you the Bible is too difficult to understand. I say there are multiple versions written in clear, modern English. We can read the Bible for our entire lives, yet still not fully understand it all. Again, I say faith begins where understanding ends. The best bible scholars don't understand it all. There are concepts that simply surpass our finite understanding.

Some things we are simply not meant to understand. Our faith begins where understanding ends.

Every day, we are faced with choices, actual forks in the road allowing us to choose God's plan or our plan for our lives. Our plan is flawed and leads to our fall. His plan is eternal life and peace. Eternal thinking takes faith in things we cannot see, hear, touch, or sense in the natural. Many of us have a small inkling of doubt, questioning whether or not everything we believe is actually real. Don't sweat it. God understands how tricky faith is for us, but we all have some faith. I've never seen air, but I

THE BATTLE GOES ON (YES, FOR ME TOO)

have faith it is there because I was told it was so. It takes faith to work a job 2–4 weeks before getting paid. You could show up on payday and the company could be gone.

I'd say it takes deeper faith to board an airplane going 30,000 feet in the air. We don't know most of the people we fly with. We've never met the air traffic control crew, mechanics, or pilot. We don't look into the pilot's eyes to see if he's had a couple drinks, or verify his credentials. Honestly, I regularly board planes without even looking to see if a pilot is even in the cockpit. A flight attendant or mechanic could've flown me (and judging by some of the rough landings, I tend to wonder) because I simply boarded the flight with faith I would get to where I was going. Not many of us would board a plane if we had no faith it would get us to our destination. When we elect to, we have faith.

We tend to cleave tightly to our earthy life, because many lack the faith to believe with 100% certainty that the vapor is not the end. Earthly life, its quality, and purpose are important. Taking care of our health can extend our vapor and help us run the race strong. Taking care of our appearance is a good thing. We shouldn't allow our bodies to prematurely decay from internal or external abuse and neglect.

That said, I find it fascinating that we will nip, tuck, and peel, fooling only ourselves into thinking that we are turning the clock back. We should live well, live healthy, and take care of our "temples" (bodies) inside and out. We must, however, realize that no matter how well we treat ourselves, the sands continue to fall through the hourglass. We will all take a final breath in the vapor. We can do every workout plan and diet (hey, I do—I want to be in good health for the remainder of the years God allows me to see), take every supplement or drug we wish. We can dig our heels in, kick, scream, and fight, but indeed our vapor will come to an end.

Faith can be a challenge, because the vapor is what is most real to the vapor mentality. We see it, feel it, smell, taste, and touch—very little faith is required to validate the vapor. The challenge arises in having the same level of faith in eternal things. The results are not always instantaneous when we have to deprogram or shift many years of thinking.

I had my "Aha!" moment with my friend, John, in a Seattle coffee shop. Yours may be happening now or it may sink in later. Others may never fully grasp this concept in their lives. But once the light bulb goes on, it doesn't necessarily stay on or stay bright. We have to make a continual effort to deprogram, refresh, and replace vapor with eternal. As we continually examine our lives, decisions, and perspective, we work on building an eternal mindset.

THE BATTLE GOES ON (YES, FOR ME TOO)

We are part spirit and flesh. We are a spirit-being having an earthly experience.

Our soul is made in the image of God. Our heart is part of the essence of who we are. Our minds guide, interpret, and navigate our flesh in our vapor. Our bodies are a shell made of physical flesh, but our souls are eternal and from God. Whether or not we acknowledge it, we all want to feel admired, loved, reassured, important, and secure.

Study the fall of satan and carefully consider his motives. Once he let insecurity into his heart, he felt his position, gifts, and talents weren't enough. Once he allowed insignificance into his heart, he wanted to take the place of God. Our carnal nature, finite minds, and earthly flesh play a game of tug-of-war with our spirit. The purpose of this life is bringing our Creator glory, loving one another, and bringing one another into closer fellowship with our Creator. God is a God of incredible Love and Grace.

Grace is the best method to help bring the vapor-minded into eternal thinking. Understanding God's grace gives us humility. His grace begins where our ability and understanding end. When we are filled with grace, our thinking becomes more selfless. We can be more patient with others and patient with ourselves. We begin to see beyond the current situation. We start to recognize the "eternity factor" in our thoughts, actions, and decisions.

I hope to have communicated to you in a manner you found loving, thoughtful, and compassionate. We all want to believe and know our lives on earth are relevant. We see our own flaws, hang-ups, and shortcomings. We see a multitude of choices before us.

God created us in anticipation that we would choose His plan for success. God sees us walking victoriously in His purpose for us, making full use of our gifts and talents. He sees us in relationship with one another. He sees Jesus as the leader and master of our lives. God sees us close to Him. He sees us viewing and navigating the vapor, destined for eternity in Heaven.

In closing, I say to you the time has come—not only to see the vapor for what it is, but for us *to see ourselves as God sees us*.

THE BATTLE GOES ON (YES, FOR ME TOO)

God, I pray that You would move by Your Spirit right now on the person reading this book. I ask that You would bring hope, joy, and love in their life. May they be stretched in their faith.

God, You gave these words to me and I glorify You for them. Without Your hand, all I do, any words I utter or write are meaningless. You alone can change hearts and lives. I pray that we who lead and we who follow would be challenged to come to You with humility and repentance. May we hunger for new understanding in You and Your purpose.

I pray You would richly bless us in all areas in this short vapor we call life. Let Your appointed purpose serve as the springboard into our eternity. We are nothing without You. I ask that eternities would be altered by what You are doing through these words and through Your power. May You receive all the glory.

I thank You for exposing the vapor for what it is. Thank You for allowing us to choose Your path, Your Love, and Your plan.

In Your Son Jesus' name, amen.

THE VAPOR

About the Author

Xola Malik is a recording artist, producer, writer, author, actor, and community servant. Under the alias "Kid Sensation," he sold over 1 million career units. In 1997, he gave his heart to Christ. Xola has produced music for major networks, sports organizations, athletes, and charities around the world. He has one prior self-published story book, *The Power of One*. The book is loosely based upon the lyrics of his song with the same title. The song and book were created to benefit *No Boundaries International,* a charity helping orphans and women who are victims of violence in the Congo, Africa. Xola's latest CD albums include *Songs for Change* and *Seasons*.

For more information, please visit:
thevaporbook.com
xolamusic.com

To have Xola speak at your special event, with your group, or to order more copies of this book, please e-mail your inquiries to:
booking4xola@gmail.com
thevaporbook.com